Countryside

by Nathan Cobb
and John N. Cole

The Stephen Greene Press
Brattleboro, Vermont

This book has been produced in the United States of America. It is designed by IRVING PERKINS ASSOCIATES, and published by The STEPHEN GREENE PRESS, Fessenden Road, Brattleboro, Vermont 05301.

Library of Congress Cataloging in Publication Data

COBB, NATHAN.
　Cityside/countryside.

　"Essays . . . written for the Boston globe's
magazine and the Maine times in 1977 and 1978."
　1. Boston—Social life and customs—Addresses,
essays, lectures.　2. Country life—Maine—Addresses,
essays, lectures.　3. Maine—Social life and
customs—Addresses, essays, lectures.　4. Cobb,
Nathan—Addresses, essays, lectures.　5. Cole,
John N., 1932–　—Addresses, essays, lectures.
I. COLE, JOHN N., 1932–　joint author.　II. Boston globe.　III. Maine times.　IV. Title.
F73.52.C62　　974.4'6104　　80–16825
ISBN 0–8289–0397–2

Contents

v

Coping 97

Getting Around 143

Foreword
by Richard M. Ketchum

LONG BEFORE there was a city, of course, there was the country. Man is said to have emerged on earth some 600,000 years ago, and for nearly all of that immense span he was a hunter and a gatherer of food. Then, about ten thousand years ago, he made one of those great leaps of which humans are capable, a leap so remarkable as to deserve the term revolution: he became a maker, rather than a taker, of food. He had discovered agriculture—the knowledge that he could sow seeds in the ground and harvest crops from them—and in so doing he unwittingly made possible the existence of cities. The farmer, in other words, by raising more food than he and his family required, freed enough of his fellows from the task of producing their own sustenance and enabled them to devote their time and energies to churches and counting houses, to arts and science and other branches of learning, and to creating the bureaucracy that seems destined to be the last survivor of human civilization. It is perhaps the ultimate irony that the farmer, who started it all, should have become in the closing years of the Twentieth Century A.D. the forgotten man, the man the rest of society neither knows nor cares much about.

Until fairly recently, the terms "country" and "farmland" were all but synonymous. The country *was* farms—and almost by definition a man who lived in the country was a farmer. But in the past four decades the wholesale industrialization of agriculture— fueled by cheap gasoline and spurred by a quest for greater profits—brought about a change from subsistence to specialization. And with it, a terrible estrangement of city and country has taken place. Before World War II, a substantial number of Americans living in cities could still recall the smells of the barnyard, the flavor of fresh whole milk and eggs, the taste of homemade butter and cheese. But no more.

The transformation of agriculture over the last forty years has exacerbated almost beyond repair the lack of understanding that always separated city and country. The vaudeville prototypes of city slicker and rube were not accidental. In America, of course, the country man was the dominant figure in society for generations. As Benjamin Franklin observed in 1784, "The great business of the continent is agriculture. For one artisan or merchant, I suppose, we have at least one hundred farmers, by far the greatest part cultivators of their own fertile lands, from whence many of them draw, not only the food necessary for their subsistence, but materials of their clothing."

In 1800—a year in which Boston had a population of 25,000—nine out of ten Americans lived and worked on farms. If you include rural areas in the calculation, an even higher percentage was involved, for nearly every villager raised some crops and livestock. Farming in that day had changed little from the ancient ways—the plowman still followed the rude instrument of his ancestors, sowed and reaped in the same manner, and cut his grain with the same curved scythe used by the Romans. Yet there was an uneasy suspicion that life might not always continue this way, and a further suspicion that if it did not, all might not go well with the Republic. Thomas Jefferson wrote to his fellow-Virginian James Madison that the United States would "remain virtuous . . . as long as agriculture is our principal object. . . . When we get piled upon one another in large cities, as in Europe, we shall become as corrupt as in Europe, and go to eating one another as they do there." Yet the continent was unbelievably bountiful; there was more free land, more good land, than recorded history could recall; and even Jefferson, looking westward, could imagine that there was "room enough for our descendants to the hundredth and thousandth generation."

In this he was badly mistaken. In the 1840's, only a single generation after Jefferson's death, Americans were inventing, adapting, and adopting the agricultural machinery that altered farm life beyond recognition, and the number of farmers required to feed the non-farming populace began dwindling from decade to decade. The productivity of the farm multiplied, the number of farmers declined, and those who remained on the land were able to supply food for all the growing cities of America, with enough to spare for export. By 1860, only five out of ten Americans worked on farms—in sixty years, that is, the proportion of those making a living from agriculture had decreased from 90 per cent to 50 per cent. By the end of the nineteenth century, the self-sufficient, diversified farm had already begun to give way to the commercialized, specialized farm, with the result that by 1980 farmers made up a mere 2 per cent of the population and were losing numbers every day.

It was no accident that the phenomenal growth of American cities occurred during the same period as labor-saving machinery and new scientific knowledge had hit the farms. Those farmers who were no longer needed to raise food because they had been replaced by machines flocked to cities in search of work—a movement that coincided with a huge influx of European immigrants, most of whom also landed in cities, and with the spread of canals, railroads, and highways, which promoted the growth of urban centers along their routes.

In New England, where the first settlers had established a pattern of agricultural villages, with the meetinghouse facing the common where everyone's livestock grazed, with meadows and cropland beginning at the edge of the back yards, the pattern began changing about the time of the American Revolution. As the villages grew, farms became more and more distant from them, and the farmer made a trip to town only when it was essential to obtain the services of a blacksmith or doctor or miller, or to buy staples from the general store. These little homesteads multiplied, their isolation increased, and each family that was thrown by necessity upon its own resources became virtually self-sufficient. The Yankee farmer, tilling his bony soil, separated even from other farmers by roads that were often impassable, tied to his land by unceasing chores, shaped a way of life around family and home that remains, to this day, a symbol of independence and self-reliance.

Eventually, of course, many of the best and most daring of the farmer's sons and daughters left for more promising lands or for less exacting toil, and a steady stream of New England youth vanished forever from the quiet villages and lonely farmsteads, bound for the prospect of fortune or adventure. The beckoning cities, for all their overcrowding and their problems, offered opportunity to the ambitious, culture and intellectual stimulation to the curious, diversity to those who had known only a numbing sameness.

Boston, which fancied itself as the hub of the solar system in Oliver Wendell Holmes's day, was often enough the city that attracted the Yankee farm boy in search of a more exciting world than he had known behind a plow. Shipping, banking, trade, medicine, education, music, art, letters—Boston had them all, then as now. And while Boston never quite achieved the rank Holmes saw for it in the solar system, there was never the slightest doubt that it was the hub of New England, the nation's only regional capital. An old man of my acquaintance still recalls standing outside his front door in a little town in southeast Vermont and watching the endless flocks of sheep pass by—thousands of animals trotting down the dusty country road, bound for Boston, 120 miles away. Today the farmers in our valley still send their milk to the Boston milkshed as their fathers and grandfathers did before them. And those same farmers, turning on the television set after evening chores are done, sit on the edges of their chairs, rooting for the Boston Red Sox, the Celtics, the Bruins, and the Patriots. For those of us who live in what is still rural New England, a trip to the city is a trip to Boston—for the Pops, the theatre, the flower show, the Museum of Fine Arts, the children's museum, the science museum, the Arnold Arboretum.

There is the rural visitor's Boston, but there is also the Boston of Nathan Cobb and the other urban dwellers, and they are by no means the same place. In this book Cobb opens our eyes to a city the visitor never really sees or quite imagines, revealing the surge of life along Boylston Street, the craft of the panhandler, the effects of a major storm on the city's heartbeat, the follies of skyscraper building. Juxtaposed against his essays are those of John Cole, speaking for and about the country, describing the slow pace of tides and seasons in a landscape peopled with marchers in a small-town parade, back-to-the-landers, the eider and the osprey, the great horned owl and the herring gull. Indeed, from the time of the earliest cities until the present, life has moved to the counterpoint suggested in these pages—to two separate melodic lines, each pursuing its own course and its own rhythm. And in Nathan Cobb's and John Cole's perceptive revelations of two disparate worlds that are as close, geographically, as Brunswick, Maine and Boston, Massachusetts, we sense the gap between their two environments and are reminded of a tale that is as old as Aesop.

The sad thing, of course, is that the City Mouse and the Country Mouse are no more able to understand each other than they were 2,500 years ago when Aesop was spinning his fables at the court of Croesus, King of Lydia. Croesus, having discovered that knowledge is power, had assembled around him those who had gained a reputation for sagacity, no matter what their nationality. It was said of Aesop, "He came to amuse, but he remained to instruct," but for all his wisdom, he came no closer than we have to bridging the gulf between country and city dweller.

You remember his story: the Country Mouse, having invited his friend from town for a visit, fed him as well as a modest larder would afford, only to have the City Mouse respond by picking at the food and remarking, "How is it that you can endure the dullness of this unpolished life? You are living like a toad in a hole." The two of them journeyed to town, where the City Mouse showed off his sumptuous quarters and fed his visitor a feast such as the Country Mouse could not have imagined. Just when the Country Mouse was beginning to enjoy his new surroundings, a rowdy party burst into the room, frightening off the mice. And no sooner had they emerged from their hiding place than they were terrorized by a pack of dogs. The Country Mouse had had enough. "Oh my good sir," he said to his friend, "this fine mode of living may do for those who like it; but give me my barley bread in peace and security before the daintiest feast where fear and care are in waiting."

During this past decade, for the first time since Thomas Jefferson's day, the tide of population movement from country to city has been reversed. The trend began during the turbulent sixties, when increasing numbers of emigrés began appearing in rural areas across the country, seeking—like the mouse—their barley bread, peace, and security, and following a path that led toward self-sufficiency. Not all of them remained, of course: the exchange of one way of life for an entirely different one is by no means easy, nor is it for everyone. But still the folk from the city come, and the drift first noted by the Bureau of the Census in 1974 has mushroomed into a nationwide movement, with all the social, political, and economic consequences that implies.

Only a handful of these migrants intend to earn a livelihood in agriculture: many are simply following the dispersal of industry to rural sections. But almost all of them, it appears, engage in some kind of after-hours work that makes them more self-sufficient than they could possibly be in a city—raising their own vegetables, keeping a few sheep or cattle or a milking goat, cutting firewood. And they are learning, in the process, what it will take to survive in the new age, where energy is no longer cheap or readily available, where a family will have to be aware of the seasons and the weather, where the most important resources are those that are renewable.

There is no telling where it will all lead, but at least a growing number of city-bred Americans will discover, at last, what the farmer has known all along—that one must work with Nature and not against her. They will learn that working on the land can be immensely frustrating and demanding, but that one may toil with dignity and independence, deriving a sense of joy and peace that has nothing to do with the material rewards. Farming, as Aesop knew, is not something that happens out there at the edge of society. It is central to society's very existence and it cannot be divorced from the rest of life.

Preface

Journey to Two Places

DESCRIBING WHAT lay beyond the doors of the home he lived in as a boy, Nathan Cobb writes: "The place was a jungle, a veritable rain forest. It would not have surprised me to have walked out the back door and met a Bengal tiger. I swear, you could actually get down on your hands and knees and watch the grass grow."

Describing the home I shared with my family from the day I was born until I reached voting age, I write of ". . . towering stone buildings without windows . . . gritty stretches of asphalt . . . a place whose inhabitants know not the phases of the moon, from which quarter the wind blows, nor the seasons of the year, and neither do they care."

Nathan, you see, was born and raised in the country (if that's what you can call what lies beyond Boston) and I arrived in my mother's bed in a fifteenth-story apartment in midtown Manhattan.

What happened after each of us had taken enough nourishment to make our own decisions is important to this book. Nathan left his green grass jungle and made his new home in the center of urban Boston, a place where he has stayed ever since— weekends included. I moved from New York City to a small, coastal community in Maine, a state that is entirely rural, offering its twenty million timbered acres to one million citizens. The entire human population of my chosen state is nearly ten times less than the number of New Yorkers now living in the city where I was raised.

I ponder often upon that data; just as I'm certain Nathan still meditates on that jungle beyond his boyhood back door. Each of us knows from whence he came; thus each of us thinks about why he left. Which is how this book came to be.

Being journalists, both of us tend to write about what's on our minds. Back there, in the distant caves of our consciousness, are questions still unanswered. Quietly, we have been seeking to resolve them for most of our adult years. Nathan wonders why he moved in the opposite direction his parents had chosen; I try to understand what prompted me to abandon a Manhattan presence three generations of my forebears had established. Our personal essays collected here are the musings of two writers whose subject is nothing less than how their lives have come to be.

It's this sort of musing that encourages attention to detail, that makes each of us take note of the minutiae of his surroundings, that provides us with our persistent enthusiasm for our environments. After all, if we chose them, if we broke away to attain them, then they must be good, they are probably better, and—in our hearts—we know they are best.

Nathan sees his city through eyes trained to observe and with convictions he himself has constructed, one after the other over the course of his independent years. The same backdrop is mirrored for me, but my setting is the opposite. Nathan's is the heart of Boston, mine is the center of coastal Maine. A reader embarking on our combined record of days is on a journey to two places, with two guides, each explaining the sights and sounds he loves best.

For Nathan, spring arrives when the Red Sox play their opening game at Fenway; for me, the season is announced by the first tremulous call of the peepers in a ditch alongside the road home. For Nathan, the city is a challenge when it comes to finding a parking space; for me, driving a car along a country lane is an exploration of solitude. Nathan is patron to the panhandler, admirer of the all-night eatery, defender of defecating dogs, and a stubborn supporter of the nation's oldest subway. I admire farmers in their fields, moose in my dooryard, terns on the wing, and the islands that scatter their solitude over my Maine horizons. Each of us, however, shares a vast affection for where we are.

The essays collected here were written for the Boston *Globe's* Magazine and the *Maine Times* in 1977 and 1978.

At one point in Nathan's and my parallel careers as *Globe* Magazine columnists, Rick Hauser, a television producer for WBGH, Boston, thought we should go visual with our opposites. Nathan and I were to meet and talk before cameras and microphones about our city/country differences. We tried two or three televised conversations, but the concept never played well in Peoria, or anywhere else. What happened when Nathan and I came together, face to face, was that each of us recognized something of himself in the other. Our "arguments" were artificial.

We had not, in our writing, been debating each other. We had written, each in his own way, about two different places. Nathan cared about one, I about the other. Writing about why you care about a place is not a contentious occupation; it's a labor of love. There is no bickering in the collection that follows. Nathan created the various topic headings; I got to write the introduction. As it has from the start, our writing has brought us together.

And, as they have from the start, our loyalties to the places we live will keep us apart. Nathan still shares his sidewalks with hundreds of thousands of Bostonians; I still watch from my windows as sea gulls soar over the trees. But wherever you live, you can recognize a part of yourself in both Nathan's world and mine.

Brunswick, Maine   JOHN N. COLE

Trends

Still Not Crazy After All These Years

A FRIEND of ours, who happens to be British, spends several months a year traveling in this country, which happens to be the United States. He usually perseveres in the cities, where, psychologically and physically unarmed, he focuses his foreigner's eye on the brooding local populace.

We always await his reports with great anticipation and amusement, viewing him as a kind of rich man's Charles Kuralt. Last year, for example, he deplaned at Logan Airport and immediately announced that Cleveland was a city in which the people seemed genuinely sorry to be alive.

Anyway, he turned up the other day, proclaiming that he was greatly relieved to be in our midst. Boston, he hurriedly explained over the bottle of warm Watney's he always carries in his slicker, was still safe. Maybe even immune, due to its geography. As for

3

the rest of the bloody mess out there in America, well, it was clear the end was somewhere at hand. Naturally, we pressed him for details as we repaired to the bar.

He first noticed it in Los Angeles, he said as he settled in, thereby immediately causing us to suspect the worst. He had checked into the Beverly Wilshire Hotel and decided to make an immediate foray into the streets in order to take the pulse of the people. He is not sure precisely when he first sensed that something was amiss, but believes it occurred as he reached Pershing Square in the downtown section after a full-length drive along Wilshire boulevard from Beverly Hills.

In any case, it soon became evident that the good burghers of L.A. (our expression, not his) were not their normal selves, whatever that is. Instead, they were acting rather starkers (his expression, not ours), which reaffirmed what we had suspected by regularly watching the 6 P.M. news.

"What became clear to me," our companion recalled in a genuinely startled tone as he reached for another beer, "is that something in their brains had snapped. Just snapped. You could see it in their eyes. Strange, faraway looks. And try to talk to them! No, you couldn't. They'd just look at you and mutter something, or start laughing wildly, or . . . or . . ." Here he began to gesture towards his throat. "Or gurgle?" we tried to help. "Right, that's it. Sort of gurgle. Right."

Our friend went on to explain that he caught the first plane out of town, which happened to take him to Phoenix. After a few days of rest and recuperation there, he took up his nomadic journey once again. Whereupon he made another startling discovery: Los Angeles was not alone. The same desperate characters were on display in San Francisco and New York, though not in Denver, Chicago or (alas) Cleveland. Something was clearly abroad in the land. But what?

At this point, our storyteller stared darkly into his brew. "It's all slipping," he said softly. "Los Angeles is only the tip of the iceberg. Try 42nd street in New York at midnight. Madness. People with

4

open wounds. Colonial outlaws. "You know, you're lucky here in Boston," he said without looking up. "I think whatever's happening out there is moving from the edge of the country toward the middle. Philadelphia will go soon. Salt Lake City. Cincinnati. Miami . . . Dallas, too . . . Detroit . . . Minneapolis . . ." We quietly arose from the table and departed, leaving our friend reciting his own private version of Rand McNally. We haven't seen him since, but trust he is in better spirits.

And he was right, of course. Boston has not developed the sense of ultimate craziness that has imbedded itself in New York and Los Angeles. Our tilt sign isn't on. Not yet. The current media/politico trick, when referring to a city which has not gone over the brink, is to call it "livable." It is not known if people such as His Honor understand the black humor inherent in literally paying tribute to the fact that you can actually remain alive in a particular city, but our friend's harrowing chronicle of three foreign ports indicates that such a criterion may be less ridiculous than we thought.

Ah, Boston: where there are no armed guards on the subway trains, no S.L.A., no Charles Manson. There is danger in the philosophy of it-can't-happen-here, but not this time. The city's Official Desperado Count is low enough to warrant confidence. On the other hand, we must always maintain a constant vigilance, lest the pendulum swing the other way and we turn into Los Angeles.

COUNTRYSIDE / TRENDS

Black Ice

I WAS a boy in grade school, skating on a suburban pond when one of the very first small doors into the natural world was opened for me. As I tussled with my schoolmates, or raced them

5

over the ice, I paused to catch my breath at an end of the pond that had hardly been skated on. There, in the clear, "black" ice I could see a small fish. I think now it must have been some sort of perch, but I am not certain. I still clearly recall, however, the silvery sides of the creature, its spot of red-orange, and the almost imperceptible movement of its feathery tail there some eight or ten inches beneath the ice, just at the line where there was a bit of water yet unfrozen.

I was flabbergasted at the sight. It had never before occurred to me that there were living creatures in the skating pond; and, most certainly, I had never imagined being able to see a fish, caught like a fly in amber, through the very ice on which I played. I watched the small creature for a long time. For reasons which have since become more clear, I was fascinated. (As I grew older, I learned that any fish could pique my fascination.) But I also felt some pity for the fish; I imagined that its crystal prison would also become its tomb, and I worried about that long after we left our games and went home for supper.

A bit later in life (and I don't think it was too long) I learned that most species of fresh water fish can survive being frozen in. As I recall it, the book I discovered told me that the creature's metabolism slows almost to a standstill in a kind of submerged hibernation. Then, when March arrives and the ice begins to soften, the fish will be freed to resume their more customary lives as bright darters among the darker waters.

As far as I know, that memory marks the beginning of my understanding that nature takes care of its own, that there is a complex, circular pattern to the seasons which—if we learn to look beyond the surface—tells us that even as we are the prisoners of winter, the plans for spring have long ago begun.

Over the years, I have learned to look for the bright signs that flash through these New England winters the way that silver fish gleamed beneath the ice. I have discovered many, but by no means all. Each year, new ones are revealed, and the mere fact of their discovery is enough to thaw the spirit and warm the heart.

6

Until I read a rather poetic botanist's journal, for example, I had never really looked at the buds on the trees that cover most of Maine, line the streets of nearly every New England town and stand like solitary soldiers on most urban parks. Like me (before my reading), you may not know that many of those buds are already alive, are already pulsing to the rhythms of spring, even though, for most of us human beings, these early days of March can seem grimmer and more wintery than any that have gone before. Our patience with snow is exhausted, our resilience to the wind has vanished; we are brittle with too much winter, bowed by the cold and yearning for a surcease that, at times, seems impossible to find.

But there is movement there, beneath the ice. As any botanist and syruper can tell you, the sap is stirring. Under the ground and beneath the bark, beyond our vision and beyond any hearing, the tree's circulation moves, drawn not by any date on our calendars, but pumped by the increasing hours of sunlight as the vernal equinox nears.

The tight parcels that have wrapped the summer's leaves and flowers since last November now swell, glisten and gain new color. Not being a botanist, I can not tell you which species does what, but I know that if you and I look, we can see the colors change, we can see some buds grow waxy, we can watch as others turn red, and there are some that fairly drip with the pressures of new life. Maple, ash, poplar, birch, beech, oak and willow—each of the deciduous trees of this region has already emerged from its winter and begun the rites of spring.

Like the fish trapped in the ice, the buds are a bright sign of survival. For us, in this region, trapped in what now seems like an endless winter, the same buds are also a message of hope and reassurance, if only we learn where to look.

7

It Doesn't Mean Beans If It's Named for Boston

RIGHT ABOUT now, in the middle of July, the intrepid Boston tourist must be ready to demand his or her money back. Sure, some of the attractions are being delivered as promised. Old Ironsides, for instance, looks a lot more authentic than anything you'll find at Disneyland. And Boston Harbor—albeit polluted—is still located on the spot where the tea was dumped.

But what about all those items that have been named after the Hub? Where are they? There may be Baltimore orioles and New York asters aboard in the land, but no city even approaches Boston when it comes to getting itself turned into an adjective. Imagine the hordes of Midwesterners and such who have arrived in town expecting each of us to be eating Boston baked beans while sitting in a Boston rocker beneath some Boston ivy with a Boston terrier at our feet.

Ha.

Some Bostonians don't know a Boston baked bean from the Hope Diamond. The little molasses-soaked things aren't even prefaced by Boston any more, the closest being those which are called New England. Even then, the last can I picked up came from Skokie, Ill. Boston brown bread isn't exactly a hometown favorite either these days, although at least one commercial variety (also dubbed New England) is canned locally. Boston lettuce, meanwhile, is grown in New England, but a lot is also grown in such diverse outlands as California and New Jersey. As for Boston cream pie—that rather untempting double layer cake with a cream or custard filling—you can usually find one particular frozen brand around town provided you don't mind the fact it comes to you from Pottstown, Pa.

Pity the poor visitor who expects Boston to be a hotbed of

8

provincial phenomena. Boston ivy is native not to the Hub but to east Asia (and is closely linked to the Virginia creeper, we might add). Then there's Boston fern. It was named in honor of the city some eighty years ago, but legend has it that the plant was actually discovered in a shipment of greenery being sent here from Philadelphia. Boston pink is another name for soapwort, a perennial herb which has become naturalized in the United States—but which originated in Europe.

The Boston terrier was actually developed here in the nineteenth century, at about the same time the first Boston rocker was built locally. Now the bad news: both are as likely to turn up in Tucumcari, N.M., as in downtown Boston. You're probably not going to find many of the locals keeping their financial records in a Boston ledger, either. The Boston bag is really a small handbag which doesn't exactly fall into the category of household item around Boston. And the Boston hooker, a different version of which exists in no small number on certain of the city's streets today, was once a popular small fishing boat. It hasn't been seen hereabouts since the turn of the century.

Nor do we Bostonians do the boston, a form of gliding, dipping waltz which no nineteenth-century Brahmin of sound mind would ever have mistaken for the more rapid Viennese. Listen, we don't even play Boston whist any more, and haven't touched the game with its two 52-card decks for more than 100 years.

As for a Boston hip . . . but what's the use? Don't bother to look around for Boston iris. Don't expect to see us dining regularly on Boston bluefish. The whole thing's a sham, a ripoff, a trick. Most of that Boston stuff isn't here any more, and some of it barely was. The Bicentennial hopeful who is searching for it deserves a refund, all right. We just hope he's smart enough to get a good Philadelphia lawyer.

What We Harvest

As imperceptibly as the days shorten, the corn tassels lengthen and New Englanders draw closer to the region's most bountiful times. The wet and stubborn ground of early May has become the plowed, seeded, cultivated and mature garden of August, about to shower us with its sweet harvest. These are the weeks of plenty, the time of the tomato, the zucchini, the yellow squash, the broccoli and the cabbage. The earliest and the newest corn arrives, its pearled kernels as tender as young grapes, its buttery sweetness tempting us to the incredible overconsumption of three, even four, ears at one sitting.

Cut worms and borers and beetles are forgotten; forgotten too are the wrenched backs, blistered hands and sweated brows that followed the long, hot hours of weeding, raking, poking, watering and loving. No calculator is put to work to total the unit cost in real estate, equipment and daily labor—the price of a tomato figured in such mere physics might be the equal of luncheon at the Ritz. And besides, this is not the place for adding machines.

It is the metaphysics of the harvest that are of such infinite value: the greater understanding of nature's miracle, the self-esteem to be found in a perfect beet grown at home, the proof of self-sufficiency, and, best of all, the unique, incredible and incomparable taste of the bounty that has been harvested, cleaned, cooked and served, gone from garden to gourmet, within a matter of hours. That aromatic and matchless moment when diner and vegetable unite, that is the moment when every garden becomes a monument, when every stooped afternoon and every raked evening becomes worth it.

We reap our August harvest with the same litany each year, with the same wonder and the same gratitude. "There is no better taste than homegrown, homecooked," we say as we down the third helping; and, of course, it is true. There can be no comparison, there is no patch of earth anywhere (and certainly not your neighbor's garden) than can produce produce as perfectly as the patch which you have plowed and planted. It is this knowledge which helps ease the blistered memories and soften the hard data of a garden's accounting.

And there is yet another harvest beyond the bounty in the steaming bowls, an August crop that has not yet been as widely recognized or praised as tomato preserves or corn on the cob. It is seldom entered in the gardener's ledgers, yet without it, there can be no proper balancing of the summer books. It is better health, and it is every gardener's heritage just as surely as calloused hands and cabbage heads.

As any medical sage will tell you, we suffer most in this nation from the afflictions of affluence. We grow obese, we get cavities in our teeth, we are prone to heart disease and hypertension because we live too well, eat too much of the wrong foods and do not get enough exercise.

We are so sorely tempted. We are bombarded, too. There is no end to the high pressure hustle on behalf of engineered foods. Every supermarket is a pageant of persuasion, every package a promise. In what other nation, at what other time in history, for example, could a multi-million-dollar industry be based on the packaging of a zero-nutrition liquid in a high-energy aluminum can to be sold precisely for what it is: a one-calorie drink that does exactly nothing for its consumer?

Ah, but the home gardener becomes a victorious rebel against the high pressure hype and the hidden persuaders of our affluent times. The hoers and rakers and stoopers and seeders get exercise along with their carrots, fresh air with their leeks and sun with their strawberries. And, when they and their families and friends enjoy the bounty of these harvest weeks, they get whole food, packaged in its skin by the miracles of natural engineering. As any nutritionist will tell you, these are the foods that nourish, these are the complete source of every somatic need.

Would you put a price on your good health? Would you set a

figure on the value of proper nutrition? Hardly. Well then, remember to enter these on your gardener's ledger and to cite them as tangible benefits when someone tells you he doesn't garden because a cellophaned supermarket tomato is so easy to come by for so little pelf.

There is more than merely the tasting of the fruits of these bountiful days for the region's gardeners. There is more, even than better health and nutrition; there is the closeness to nature that every gardener has earned, and never is the nearness more sweet than it is during these weeks of shortening days and lengthening corn tassels.

CITYSIDE / TRENDS

Voices for Any Mood or Occasion

How could Alexander Graham Bell have seen it coming? He naturally assumed people were going to use his wonderful invention to talk to each other. There was simply no predicting the twentieth century, when mankind would combine the telephone with the tape recorder and come up with voices in the night.

They are out there waiting for you to dial. Janet Christenson has honeydew melon prices. James Anderson is poring over the Book of Acts. Dorothy Thomas is checking her wind instruments. So never mind that people on the block seem not to notice you, because for a few message units a day you can have more friends than you need. In and around Boston, all manner of folks are waiting to bend your ear.

You want Weather? Who doesn't? Ms. Thomas and her friends are at the standard 936–1234, but if the lines are clogged and you're being overcome with an uncontrollable urge to know whether the barometer is rising or falling, there is always 567–4670. In the meantime, the marine forecast at 569–3700 will keep you posted on white whales and such. My own personal favorite is the aviation weather report at 569–1773, possibly because I have always secretly possessed an intense curiosity about Boston-to-Albany route winds.

Fine, but what about Venus? Mars? Orson Welles? Access to the heavens is through 491–1497. This "recorded earth and space report" would seem to cover everything, but apparently not. It excludes the other-worldly MBTA, the daily condition of which is found at 722–5050. This message—which actually sounds as if it were taped in Park Street Under—neglects to suggest methods of assistance to those commuters setting out on the Green Line. Luckily there is Dial-A-Prayer, at 524–3133. The last time I checked here, one James Anderson was verbally trailing the disciple Paul through Corinth, which he—Anderson, not Paul—likened to the Combat Zone in Boston. The tale depressed me so much that I immediately rang up Dial-A-Pickle Joke at 426–6655. "Who is pickle enemy number one?" the manic voice asked. "*Dillinger!*" I bellowed, and immediately felt better.

If you're big on lists of what's going on, there is Jazz Line at 262–1300 and Arts Line at 261–1661. (The Bicentennial's "Boston 200" line—338–1775—has lately been going unanswered. Does that mean the Bicentennial is finally over?) Personally, I try not to miss the daily Fish Landings and Prices, 542–7878, as read by a male voice straight from "Candlepins for Cash." To my way of thinking, it clearly tops Janet Christenson at the toll-free Shopping Guide for Consumers, 800–392–6026. Of course, it depends on whether you're into ocean perch or Italian prune plums.

Dialing for the birds is just the thing if you can't get to the local marsh. Good news from the Voice of Audubon at 259–8805: no fewer than fifteen long-billed dowagers and seven red-breasted nuthatches were recently spotted on Plum Island. But don't celebrate with a cigarette. The Smokers Dial Message at 665–6200, insists upon a combination of resistance and divine aid to rid you of the poisons in your body. You might try verse instead. Phone-A-Poem, 492–1144, offers assistance such as "October Song" and "Dipping In." Sometimes it even invites you to recite your own poem at the sound of the beep. Resist temptations to breathe heavily in iambic pentameter.

Finally, if you think you've won the lottery, call 575–1000 for recorded confirmation. When you discover you've lost again, you can curse the messenger at will, secure in the knowledge you won't be answered back. That, of course, is an added benefit of having a machine at the other end of the line. All it takes to reach this whirring shoulder to cry on is a dime and a little time. Time? That's 637–1234.

COUNTRYSIDE / TRENDS

Woodstoves and the Technological Fix

I FEEL a fluttering of apprehensions when I read that woodstoves are not only being more stringently and scientifically analyzed, but that my chemist friend Sam Butcher is in the process of researching the possibility that wood smoke may be an air pollutor of considerable significance.

I don't want to learn the results of that research. I know that's an immature and irresponsible statement, but it is also true. I have often thought of myself as being a "transitional man," a person born into the peaking of the industrial age and living out his years at the start of the post-industrial society. I have decided I like the role. For one thing, it allows me to be immature and irresponsible. There is always the excuse that I am too tossed in the vortex of turbulent cultural change to really know what I'm talking about or doing with my resources.

I do not, for example, want to get too scientific or efficient about woodstoves. What's happening, you see, is that folks locked in their allegiance to the infallibility of the "technological fix" are now trying to apply that fix to devices as relatively primitive and non-technological as the woodstove. I want nothing to do with it.

I like woodstoves because they dry wet socks, or scorch them, better than any other heat source known. I like them because the smoke smells great when the stove is lit, and because there is no other BTU producer that is as friendly, as reassuring, as contenting and as drowsy as a woodstove on a winter afternoon.

I like woodstoves because I love what they burn. Pine, popple, red oak, white oak, maple, birch, beech, butternut, ash . . . where would I have learned so much about the wonder of wood if not for woodstoves. (You'll notice, I did not mention elm—an omission every stovewood splitter would applaud.) Now where would I have made that fine discovery if it had not been for woodstoves? And how would I have been persuaded to leave the Giants and the Redskins and the Patriots struggling on their Astroturf while I walked in the frozen forest to buck a windfall oak with enough cordwood in its two-century bulk to keep our family warm for a month; how could that possibly have happened were it not for woodstoves?

I don't want to know what's scientifically efficient. I like learning what burns longest, or fastest, or poorest, and I like learning on my own, with poker in hand and curse on lips as I pummel a faltering fire back to life and promise myself I'll never try green elm again, even if it is free for the asking. Nor do I want to have to post a logarithmic table by the stove to tell me what amount of BTU's I'm getting with the draft open or shut, how much soot is sticking to the chimney, or what the radiant heat quotient might be. What I like is a roaring fire when we feel like it, and a gentle one when we're in a gentle mood. To hell with what's efficient.

There's nothing efficient about woodstoves; it's the wrong word for them. They are sometimes a pain in the neck; they are more often balm for the soul. But now that heating oil prices are

15

beginning to compete with the price of good Scotch whiskey and the spectre of oil-less winters is upon us, we are pulling woodstoves from the nineteenth century into the twentieth and lathering them with our twentieth-century precision. It's the same approach that has all but ruined the notion of romantic love, brought us free verse, blob art, and an end to sentimental marriage. If we analyze too much and too well, we elminate every abstract, and without abstracts there is no romance, and without romance there is, as far as I'm concerned, little point to this earthly journey.

The trend, however, is against me. Not just with woodstoves, but with other alternate systems as well. Now they are vibrating computers into nervous breakdowns trying to get them to compute the precise amount of sunlight that must enter a home to give it the precisely right amount of solar energy to heat the place at maximum efficiency. (That word is everywhere.)

I didn't know anything about computers when we built our home, and I'm glad I didn't. They tell me now we have too many windows, that it's inefficient. Well, we have other rewards that still can't be computed. We have the celestial vista and its soothing wisdoms to feed our souls, and so what if there is too much glass. It gives us sustenance that can't be measured until someone invents calipers for the human spirit. I'm a transitional man, remember, an old fogey too far gone to care about wood smoke pollution and solar efficiency, and I'm absolutely delighted at my timing.

There's a Horse in the Living Room

ON ONE hand, things may not be as bad here as in other cities. In New York last February, for instance, officials who heard a strange clomping sound behind an apartment door found a horse on the other side. In Fort Wayne, a month later, a fire inspector ventured into the cellar of a pet store and discovered eighty alligators, fifty poisonous snakes, hundreds of rats and mice, a gila monster, and a large dog.

On the other hand, the way things are going my neighborhood may someday look like the cellar of a certain pet store in Fort Wayne. Now I have nothing against pets, you should understand. Several cats have been domiciled in my various past homes, and I can honestly say that I believe a well-bred Irish Setter to be among the very best of man's friends. It's just that if there is any truth to reports that the Carnation Co. has been testing a contraceptive dog food I hope a few hundred truckloads find their way into Boston before a Saint Bernard is elected mayor and appoints a Great Pyrenees police commissioner.

Anyone who crams a huge dog into an apartment is not beyond believing that a gila monster might make a fun roommate. I once had a city friend who owned what was surely the world's largest German shepherd. It looked like a furry hippopotamus. When I jokingly asked if the dog was afraid of the owner or anything else, my friend was ready with a serious answer. "He's not afraid of me," he replied, "but he's scared of my boa constrictor." *Your boa constrictor!* It also turned out that the dog didn't cotton to burglars either, because shortly thereafter he watched three of them ransack the apartment without so much as lifting a meaty paw.

Which brings me to academia's reason for what Newsweek magazine will surely someday be calling "the urban pet explo-

17

sion." It goes something like this: as alienation increases within the inner city, residents are seeking a dependable source of warmth and contact. Well, maybe so. I sometimes get lonely when there is no one else home, but I must admit that it never occurred to me, as it did to that New York apartment dweller, to fill the living room with a horse. And I should also point out that most of the Doberman Pinschers with which I have come in contact have not struck me as being either dependable or warm. If (as one sociologist has pointed out) a dog can be looked upon as a "non-demanding, non-critical friend," then I can only surmise that such an observer has not yet seen a Russian Wolfhound drag its owner across Boston Common in a frantic effort to stretch its legs after a day locked inside a studio apartment.

Large dogs in the city are a classic ego trip. Dog-walkers are a cliquish, clannish bunch who compare their charges as if the animals were children. They virtually take over Commonwealth avenue and the Esplanade during the day, chatting in small groups while their pets either 1) strut, 2) pose, 3) defecate, or 4) terrorize passersby. One Boston owner of a large dog recently stated that his pet takes the threat out of meeting human beings. I'm sure it does, but I'm also sure this particular person has problems with human relationships which are even larger than his bill for dog food.

John Steinbeck, once observing apartment dogs and their owners on the streets of New York, came to the conclusion that man and beast living together in such situations come to resemble each other. "They grow to walk alike," he pointed out, "and have the same set of head." This is not a new notion, of course, but it may say something about the egos and fantasies of certain city people. Why else would anyone own both a one-bedroom apartment and an Afghan hound if not to attempt to osmose a bit of style from the luckless beast?

Two and one-half years ago there was a terrifying incident involving a 200-pound Saint Bernard which lived in a basement apartment on Beacon Hill. It seems that the enormous animal—

for some unfathomable reason, according to police—turned on its owner and some of her acquaintances, mauled them, and literally had to be gunned down on the street outside. It was a sad story, but it never would have happened if the people had owned a horse instead.

COUNTRYSIDE / TRENDS

The Continental Shelf, and Me

THE DORY will have to be hauled out soon. The job is no trouble. This boat is so light, so finely fashioned that a person just a bit more muscular than I could carry it on his shoulders like a portaged canoe. This dory's portability is one of the reasons I acquired her in a kind of exchange several years ago. For more than a decade before that, I had another dory. (I have owned dories of one sort or another for the past thirty years.) That one was a stout and rugged craft, a chore for four hefty men to move.

I traded her for the newer model because her stoutness made it difficult for me to launch her on a whim, or row her as easily as I thought I would like. The new boat was acquired because she was designed to be everything the older one was not. Built of the sprightliest white cedar, fitted with hand-turned spruce oars and fashioned to the smallest possible dimensions which would still allow her to function as a dory, the new boat was created for one person—myself.

There is a reason for that. I passed the mid-century mark on my personal calendar just about the time the new dory came along, and I acquired her as a lure to exercise. With what the children call my "continental shelf" expanding at a noticeable rate over my belt-line, I had to agree that some sort of prolonged conditioning

19

was essential if I were to maintain any sort of semblance of "shape." I was, quite definitely, getting out of shape.

I had tried jogging. All it took was once to convince me there were no entertainment possibilities in that particular form of conditioning. As a former distance runner I should have known that only the hope of glory could keep me trotting along lonely roads. I tried walking, because I had read somewhere that walking is a fine kind of exercise. Well, I like walking, but not as a chore that must be fulfilled. Then came a stab at tennis—a throwback to another stage of my youthful past. I pulled a muscle trying to serve an ace to son Bob who was defeating me and I retired in grave pain.

The choice of rowing became inevitable. I had rowed for years in the course of making my living as a fisherman; it is a solitary pastime and I like being alone on the water. Also, if I took along my fishing tackle, what had begun as a spasm of self-improvement might be transformed to sheer pleasure by the arrival of a school of stripers.

Eight months went by, one rowing season from March through October, and I might have pulled a mile or so across the cove and back. "That dory is too heavy," I rationalized whenever the children and The Boss chided me and my continental shelf.

Thus the new boat—as graceful, as pleasing, as able and capricious a one-person dory as you are ever likely to find. And here it is October, our last rowing month in Maine, and I must review a summer when I dreamed of rowing more than I ever really rowed. Ten miles, no more, did I take that lovely dory. Each mile was sheer joy, there is no doubting that. I can remember nearly every foot. I can see the young eiders diving off the bow, recall the osprey on its island nest, chuckle at the curious seal who followed me a mile or two, bemused, I suppose, at the sight of a grown man shouting self-encouragement as he bent to his oars.

There was nothing disagreeable in any aspect of the dory; I was charmed by every moment with her. Why, then, did I not row more often? Why, then, have I done little (well, nothing) to lessen

20

the stress of my waistline against my belt? Why, then, haven't I done more to build muscle tone, to restore some of my youthful sinews, to get in better shape?

I claim it is the press of my work. There is nothing but pudginess to be earned from hours at the typewriter, flabbiness from holding a telephone, and a broadness in the seat from driving a car from one event to another. Yet these are the hallmarks of my trade. Where do I find the time for rowing?

Don't answer. I know. I could get up an hour earlier each morning, or row a half-hour before supper each evening. Indeed, those are the best times for light air and calm water. I did not use them, and now the dory must come out—an act which faces me with the irrevocable evidence of my failings and the bulging witness of my continental shelf.

I shall order a half-cord of uncut and unsplit logs. Once they are dumped in the middle of the drive, I must exercise or freeze . . . or ask one of the boys to saw and split.

CITYSIDE / TRENDS

In Pursuit of Junk Chic

CHECKING OUT the "suburban news" (a contradiction of terms if ever there was one), we find that certain communities beyond our urban borders are considering proposals to limit the number of so-called garage sales in their midst. Fat chance. The garage sale—or yard sale in less prosperous locales—is the hottest thing to hit the suburbs since Tupperware. But it has done more than simply reaffirm P.T. Barnum's law that sixty new suckers inevitably join us every hour. It has created a whole new fad.

Junk chic.

In the old days, meaning the 1960s, your social worth was measured by your access to hotshot political radicals. Then came rural consciousness and its visible symbol, the pick-up truck. Now, status is a fifteen-year-old toaster with one of its heating coils missing. One simply has to keep up, doesn't one? If people are willing to pay $35 for new jeans that are supposed to look like old jeans, imagine the market for the real thing. Anything and everything is sought, from busted bun warmers to partial Parcheesi sets. The result is a kind of overground junk network, with people moving bits of rubbish around to one another as if the items are works of art. Collecting junk is the new American luxury, not unlike collecting paintings. Really, my dear, you should stop by sometime and see my souvenir wastebasket of Florida.

My friend Randy goes to garage sales. Hundreds of them. This is his best time of year ("Spring cleaning," he points out), his weekends chock full of junk. He doesn't have a system. He simply drives his Mercedes Benz lazily through the suburbs until he spots a sign on a tree. Then he follows the hastily crayoned arrows until he finds himself knee deep in Whiffle Balls and electric can openers. "After a hard week at the office," he maintains, "there's nothing quite like going out on a Saturday and buying an old garden hose. It makes you glad to be alive."

Last year Randy's prizes included a Holiday Inn flyswatter, a Mickey Mouse figurine, and the caboose to a Lionel train set. He brought them back to his apartment in the city, where they occupy a prominent place near his valuable etchings. This year he is hot on the trail of a Flexible Flyer and a mashie niblick. Randy, by the way, earns in excess of $60,000 per annum.

Environmentalists naturally applaud people such as this. Psychologists, meanwhile, have begun to ponder their motives. One acquaintance in the analysis game has revealed to me that she believes Randy and his ilk are suffering guilt over their increasing wealth and are subconsciously trying to recapture their days of financial insecurity. As one who experiences financial insecurity rather regularly, I must hasten to inform Randy of its drawbacks.

Of course, there are many people who aren't into junk chic. Not intentionally anyway. They're the same ones who never enjoyed the brief company of radicals during the 1960s, and if they own pick-up trucks it's because they use them in their work. These are the folks for whom junk isn't an alternative, but a necessity. They buy plastic chaise lounges because that's what they can afford. They are the middlemen, warehousing the stuff for a few years, providing the age and wear so necessary to bring a good price in the marketplace. Unlike the garage sale devotees who view junk as a part-time hobby, these folks endure it as a full-time life.

The motives of the hinterland town fathers in proposing to limit the number of garage sales are unclear. Perhaps they don't want their tree-lined streets turned into arcades which hustle coffee percolators and plastic dishes. Maybe the local merchants view junk as a threat. In any case, the quest for old pieces of nothing marches on through the suburbs, a splendid heir to the Hula-Hoop. Hula-Hoop? That's fifty cents, please, cash and carry.

COUNTRYSIDE / TRENDS

Confessions of an Auction Addict

THERE IS no end to what you can learn about yourself. If anyone had told me just a few years back that I could be absolutely obsessed by auctions, I would have dismissed the notion as fantasy.

Well, all that has changed. Not only do I find myself going completely bananas at auctions, but I must declare that the process of bidding sets me to trembling, causes my heart to pound so I'm afraid it's going to explode through my shirt, and so upsets my emotional equilibrium that I find I can not sleep the night before an auction and need hours of aimless activity to make my re-entry to the real world after I've spent any time listening to an auctioneer's song of acquisition.

In one sense, my obsession is all Maine's fault. I am convinced there is no other state in the nation where auctions of such depth, such splendor and such economy are held. It has to do with the state's maritime and agricultural heritage. The dynasties that evolved in coastal Maine during the days when the state's great sailing ships dominated the oceans of the world are dynasties of collectors. How could a sea captain or ship owner prove his worth if he did not bring home a Ming vase from China, a Limoges cup from France, or have his ship's carpenters make him a fine pine chest, or a cherry desk for his lady? Or how could a farmer keep a well-stocked barn if he did not fill it with hand-carved hay rakes, lovingly fashioned grain scoops, and baskets woven of sweet grass?

There is simply not another state which so combines the sea and the land with the socio-economic timing that saw the shipping-farming economy peak about a century ago. As the graceful wooden ships gave way to iron uglies, and as supermarkets shut down self-sufficient farms, the possessions of those vanishing eras were assembled in the homes of the heirs to the Maine that once had been. There they stay, locked in the vaults of family pride and happy memories, many of them still performing the services for which they were so carefully fashioned.

Until a dynasty metamorphoses, either because its lineal descendants lose interest, move away or simply peter out; then come the auctioneers. None that I have encountered in Maine is better, more considerate and more honest than F.O. Bailey of Portland—a firm that's been around as long as most of the dynasties whose collections it auctions off. F.O. Bailey folks treat the accessories of another century with a kind of artless and genuine respect; no false awe, but no patronizing either.

Which is another special characteristic of Maine. Where else could you find a company as mellow as F.O. Bailey? Where else could you come across an auctioneer like Frank Allen who combines his true Yankee accent with his equally pure Yankee humor and makes every auction great entertainment, whether or not you get into the bidding.

But, of course, I do get into the bidding. I can not help myself, any more than I can hold my breath when Tracy puts the spring's first mayflowers under my nose. It's not that I go to these auctions needing anything. Aside from refills for my pocket pens—which are forever running dry at journalistic moments of crisis—there isn't much I *need* these days. But when Frank Allen starts talking about the merits of a hand-made wooden snow shovel that must be at least seventy-five years old and was fashioned by a Maine farmer who used only his axe and pocketknife to sculpt an object of amazing grace, why then my resistance vanishes, my acquisitive pulses pound, and, as the saner members of our household will tell you, I take leave of my composure and my senses.

Once the lust for possession rages, there are no bounds on my determination and eagerness. I bid when I need not bid, I brook no opponents. No sooner does a competitor get a bid voiced, but my higher one comes booming. It matters not if the Budget Director's hand is tugging at my arm or trying to wrest my auction card away; I will not be dissuaded. Frequently I have raised my very own bids, so frantic is my compulsion. (In which case Frank Allen pretends not to notice my confusion and gently repeats my lower bid as if I hadn't erred.)

I write this in the depths of my latest trauma. Frank and the entire F.O. Bailey crew have been just seven miles from here in Bath for the last four days. Do you have any idea what that can do to an auctionholic? A four-day auction—I need succor, I am undone. It will take me a year to recover. How have I come to this; who, most of all myself, would have thought it possible?

But please stop by and see the all-brass gooseneck lamp on my desk. They don't make them like this anymore.

The Ten-Thousand-Dollar Parking Space

As CRAZY as it sounds, it always seemed inevitable. The day was simply bound to come. No matter what had to be overcome—including insurance and theft rates that defy reason—Bostonians simply refused to relinquish their automobiles. The MBTA offered little relief, though it is unlikely that even a subway system which travels at the speed of sound could wrench locals from the driver's seat.

But really now . . . condominiums for cars?

By God, yes. The news comes from the Brimmer Street Garage, a somewhat exclusive hostelry for motorized vehicles which is located on what is called the "flat" of Beacon Hill, a somewhat exclusive hostelry for human beings. Having found themselves operating in the red, the owners of the garage have decided to sell parking spaces in the same way real estate brokers sell apartments. An apartment, of course, would cost you more money. But not much.

Let's see now. Prices for parking "units" at Brimmer street range from $7000 to $25,000, but there's really no need to be ostentatious. I mean, I could live happily with a "small car" space, ten of which are available on the first floor for $10,000 each. "Small car" isn't defined in the company's sales brochure, but I have the feeling I will have no difficulty meeting the criteria. Whether or not my rather faded foreign transportation system will meet with the approval of other owners, however, is another question. I can already hear them muttering: "There goes the neighborhood."

But this is America after all, and my car has as much right to live there as does theirs. Provided I can pay the freight. In addition to my $10,000 purchase price, I am told to expect first-year realty tax and common charges totalling $1454.06. That's *now,* and I haven't heard Mayor Kevin White (who lives a block from the garage, incidentally) saying he expects the city's tax rate to plummet in the near future. Assuming I finance 80 percent of the purchase price at 8.75 percent over ten years, I can also expect to pay another $100.27 per month in principal and interest. All of which means that after estimated first-year deductions of $378.10, I find I can park my "small" car for twelve months for an out-of-pocket cost of $2279.16—or $189.93 per month.

I know, I know. You are thinking that there are sections of Boston where you can comfortably house a family of four for that kind of money. But, really now, what's more important, a man's children or his car? Why, $2279.16 is almost $300 less than a year of room and board at Harvard. A veritable bargain.*

"It's a luxury, quite clearly," understates Scott Donahue, who has been selling the condominiums for the Brimmer Street Garage Corporation. "It's marketability isn't as an investment. People are buying convenience, service and security. Of course, to people who have a lot of money, perhaps those things aren't luxuries. Many people who are wedded to their cars might think they're necessities."

Donahue, a student at Suffolk Law School, sounded almost apologetic for selling "small car" parking spaces for $190 a month. Quite frankly, I don't see how the Brimmer Street Garage Corporation could resist the temptation. After all, there was a waiting list for their spaces when they were renting at a mere $65 to $90 a month.

"Still, I'm not sure the owners were sure people would pay this much for parking," Donahue informs. "They knew the spaces were expensive and they knew Boston was fairly provincial." Not to worry. Within a month of being put on the market, twenty-three of the garage's sixty-six units had been sold. As crazy as it sounds.

*NOTE: This was written in September of 1977. Here, and elsewhere, the astute reader in 1980 will, of course, double the interest rate quoted, and increase the other figures by a like factor. The author reports that the only cost in Boston that has gone *down* in three years is the re-sale value of his automobile. THE PUBLISHER

The Real County Fair

THE FAIR season here in Maine is approaching its crescendo. Yes, it is a lovely time of the year, but the "fair" I have in mind has more to do with county fairs, agricultural fairs, state fairs . . . you know, the ones with midways, horse racing, girlie shows, and the exhibits of prize winning canteloupes, peach preserves, patchwork quilts, and turkeys tall enough to knock a large man down.

There was a time there, even in this rural corner of the northeast, when the genuine agricultural fair—the county fair as it was always intended to be—appeared to be an endangered species on its way to extinction. As more and more small farms were abandoned, as barns collapsed and deserted farmhouses fell into their own cellar holes, the agricultural fair became a travesty of what it once had been. In spite of holdouts like the Grange and the Ladies Horticultural Society, there just wasn't enough interest in who could grow the largest Hubbard squash, or crochet the most intricate antimicassars. Fairs became sites for midways, roller coasters and cotton candy instead of contests among Plymouth Rocks and bantam roosters.

Thank goodness the pendulum is swinging in the other direction. The avalanche of abandonment has slowed; the small farm is gradually being restored to a position of some significance in the region's economy. Not only are some of the most stubborn of the oldtimers finding it a bit less difficult (and farming has never been easy) to hang on, but a new breed of young people seem determined to make a go of it on the land, no matter how many winters they have to battle, or how many droughts they must endure.

As the cost of shipping a bunch of carrots from California continues to climb at ever accelerating speeds, the benefits of buying home-grown vegetables at the local farmer's market are becoming more and more apparent to greater numbers of con-

28

sumers. In another generation or so, as the cost of energy and the need to conserve it become convincing arbiters of socio-economic change, it's a sure bet the small farm will continue to play a more and more important role.

Which pleases me for a number of reasons, not the least of which is the concurrent restoration of the agricultural aspects of New England's agricultural fairs. I'll never forget the first time I wandered off the midway of the Sagadahoc County Agricultural and Horticultural Society's annual extravaganza. I found myself in a long, cavernous wooden building; both sides and a double aisle down the middle were lined with the creations of the Society ladies: jars of royal purple grape preserves, sienna pumpkin pies; golden loaves of home-baked bread; ruby red currant jelly; blueberries too plump for their baskets, and hanging from the walls were tumbling tapestries of country colors gathered into patchwork quilts I had seen before only in pictures.

I was all but alone in that barn of a building. I could hear the sounds of the midway and the cheering of the trotting race crowds as the afternoon sun spilled through the few high windows. A woman out of the past, with a true poke bonnet on her head, sat by one of the booths; she'd brought in her peach pies, and she was going to stay with them. I realized then that what was going on outside had little or nothing to do with what these country fairs were meant to signify. In the midst of that abundant harvest and those colorful testimonies to inspired toil, I began to understand what fairs were meant to be about.

That was nearly twenty years ago. In the interim, the kind of display that proved so unforgettable for me became less and less a part of the fair season, until about four or five years back. Then, lo and behold, the heritage of the harvest began to be restored. And last year, in a meadow not far from Maine's capital, the Maine Organic Farmers and Gardeners Association sponsored a country fair that paid most of its attention to produce and how to grow it, as opposed to midways and how to make a fast buck. That fair was such a success, they're going to do it again this year.

What's happened is that a new generation of young people has discovered the last of the oldtime farmers, and the meeting of the two has been beneficial for all of us as well as both of them. When the "back to the land" movement began a decade or so ago, a good many forecasters predicted early failure. Well, the restoration of the country fair is witness to success, and I'm delighted that the season is in full stride.

CITYSIDE / TRENDS

A Down-to-Earth Hobby

BASICALLY, THERE are only three items which are indispensable to living in downtown Boston: a parking space, a friend or relative at City Hall, and a telescope. The first is hoarded and the second is flaunted. But the third . . . well, let's just say that the third is not yet completely out of the closet.

New Yorkers, of course, are totally guiltless about their voyeurism. It is not unusual to visit an apartment in Manhattan and find a pair of binoculars resting on each and every window sill. And you may be certain they are not used for picking out Scarlet Tanagers, although a New York friend likes to joke about seeing several Common Loons and American Coots from his bathroom window.

Bostonians are more circumspect. "Ah, yes," they are likely to reply when guests point out that a telescope seems a bit out of place in a basement apartment, "Jupiter's satellites are positively stunning these days." To say nothing of the tenant across the street.

Buying one's first telescope, then, is a bit like attending one's first pornographic movie. Several discreet strolls past the sales counter must be taken before a query is posed. "Say, I've been thinking about one of these things for the kids," the prospective buyer finally opens.

"For astronomical or terrestrial observations?" the salesman asks, quickly getting to the heart of the matter.

This is the moment of truth. If the buyer reveals his intentions he will be riddled with shame. If he doesn't, he may go home with a facsimile of the Palomar Observatory under his arm.

"Terrestrial," he mumbles, looking around to make sure no one can overhear him. The salesman smiles, knowing that he need not be bothered delivering his speech about image brightness, resolving power and field of view.

Many telescopes come with little booklets which are chock full of helpful hints such as the fact that magnifying power is equal to the focal length of the objective divided by that of the eyepiece. To the urban astronomer, this is about as important as the expected agricultural growth of Paraguay. The only thing he really wants to know is if the thing will sufficiently magnify the person in the third window from the left on the fifth floor. Jupiter's satellites, indeed.

However, as Raymond Burr convinced Jimmy Stewart in "Rear Window," keeping tabs on the neighborhood can have its drawbacks. On the other hand, the interest in optical devices in the city has undoubtedly created a whole class of actors and actresses who are just waiting to be discovered behind the Venetian blinds.

And who knows where it can lead? There is one gentleman in town who recently felt a particular urge to keep an eye on a rather attractive neighbor. After hemming and hawing at a local discount house, he returned home one day with a 30-power telescope. He calmly waited for nightfall, unpacked the carton and turned down the lights. He set up the tripod. After mastering the focusing, he carefully aimed the device at a dimly lit window in the distance. He focused again. Suddenly everything he could see was completely sharp.

And there in the eyepiece was his neighbor looking back at him through a telescope.

31

"What Do You Do for Exercise in Maine?"

COMPULSIVE RUNNING has affected so many of my urban and suburban acquaintances that I begin to wonder if it hasn't reached the point of becoming a national epidemic. No matter where I stay on my infrequent visits to the paved places of New England, I can count on being surprised by the disappearance of my host (or hostess) just when I am set for a succulent breakfast. Instead, my breakfast suppliers are slipping out their door, clad in mod sweat suits and tricky shoes of many colors. "I'm going for my run," they explain. "I'll be back in awhile." And return they do, puffing and snorting and exhibiting their now redolent costumes as if sweat suits have become the equivalent of a teacher's gold star.

Meanwhile, demonstrating prowess I never display at home, I've gotten my own breakfast and, as I enjoyed it, pondered the mystery of why so many otherwise sensible folk in Brunswick or Portland and their counterparts have taken to trotting along the roadsides every morning of every season of the year, including even these snowstruck days of January. Why I can remember it was just a few years ago that the solitary jogger who bumped by our house every morning acquired a townwide notoriety for his running penchant. "The Jogger," we called him, enunciating and accenting the title with just enough of a sneer so every listener would know that although the fellow was mannered and harmless, he was also considered a bit daft.

That daffiness is now nationwide apparently, save but for me. As a former distance runner in school and college I had quite enough, thank you, of cramped muscles, shin splints, violent nausea, thumping heart, and the labored breathing that are the hallmarks of running—not to mention the denial (significant in those days) of between-meal snacks, smoking, drinking and, for some ardent coaches, any contact with the opposite sex more strenuous than conversation. Why anyone would take on such burdens, voluntarily and at an age when wisdom is supposed to prevail, is quite beyond me. It must, I have decided, be the result of the urban and suburban environment—an aspect none of us yet comprehends.

With these opinions stacked as carefully as split kindling in my skull, I was, nevertheless, caught short by the inquiry of a city folk with whom I recently shared a short auto trip. He, fresh from his "run" with face a-crimson and cheeks aglow turned to ask, "And what do you do for exercise during the winters in Maine?"

I thought briefly of responding: "Well, I sure ain't dumb enough to trot along snowy roads in my union suit," but courtesy prevailed. What I said was, "I chop a little wood."

"Oh," said my passenger, "that's good for the muscle tone," nodded his head approvingly and apparently has gone through the rest of his life with happy visions of me staying "in shape" bent over a bucksaw in front of a 15-foot logpile.

What I said was, "chop a little wood," and I meant just that: I chop as little wood as I possibly can, and when I do take axe in hand, it is only to chop the little wood—the small bits of pine kindling that help get the stoves started. The heavy stuff I leave to Sam (who is already so in shape he would never consider his chores as conditioning) and think of my part of the job as organizational. I tell him where to stack the results of his labors. If Sam is playing hockey, or whatever, I lean on Marshall, and if he is absent, any likely looking neighbor lad I can collar.

I do keep the bird feeders filled; I help push cars when they are stuck in the snowbanks (provided the autos are compacts), and on Saturdays, weather permitting, I walk to the end of the drive to get the mail. On Tuesdays I take out the garbage for the town truck to pick up. Some afternoons, if I mistime my arrival, I help carry in groceries. I will carry in the snow shovels from the barn for anyone who wants to test them, but most of the time these days

I sit around wondering why so many folks are running. It's a tiring thought that, I'm certain, helps to keep me in shape.

Boston's Ultimate Game

THE PARTY'S over, in more ways than one. If you feel the symptoms of a hangover on this first morning of 1977, your infirmity may be due to something other than New Year's residue. Let's face it: we're going to miss not having 1976 to kick around anymore. For better or for worse, the never-ending events of the Bicentennial gave us something to talk about, even if they didn't always live up to their advance billing. Among the astonishing wonders awaiting Boston in 1977 are Park Plaza (probably), fifteen city councilors instead of nine (possibly), and another madcap scheme to improve traffic at Charles Circle (inevitably). It's all enough to make you pull up the covers and go back to sleep.

But wait. Word has reached us of a marvelous scheme being hatched within City Hall. It would have been announced sooner, but the messenger has been lost in the building's maze of corridors since Thursday morning. In any case, the plan is designed to both rekindle the spirit of '76 (see how freely promotional copy drips from the pen?) and rescue Boston from its precarious financial position. It also will hasten the overhaul of city government, different plans for which seem to be in the minds of half the politicians in town.

The idea is called Mayor '77, and it is so simple that it is actually no surprise that the city fathers and mothers didn't conceive it sooner. Briefly stated, Boston will celebrate the coming Fourth of July by running a giant lottery, the winner of which will immediately be inaugurated—as if you haven't already guessed by the snappy title—Mayor '79, Mayor '81, etc.

The revenue-raising potential of the plan is mind-boggling. If people will pay the Commonwealth of Massachusetts fifty cents for a shot at a measly $1 million in The Game, how much will they pay for the chance to be able to afford the steaks at DeLuca's Market on Charles street? Of having three drivers, all of whom are police detectives? Of going to Stanley Cup games for free, and possibly even sitting with the state treasurer? The billions taken in by Mayor '77 might even be enough to keep the city's tax rate under $300 next year, though no one in City Hall is yet ready to make such an optimistic prediction.

But think of the excitement and pride that will be carried over from 1976! It will be as if the tall ships never raised anchor. We can't, of course, expect the Queen herself to return to our humble shores in this century, but perhaps the promise of being able to tie up her horses in the Public Garden could entice Princess Anne to the drawing. Which will be held, as it should be, atop the gently swaying John Hancock Tower, complete with Howard Cosell, Walter Cronkite, and satellite coverage. It is only fitting that the winning number be drawn by the Hon. Kevin H. White, in whose name two million tickets have already been pledged by unnamed real estate developers.

And let us not overlook the potential excitement of having a completely unknown face beaming out from behind the mayor's desk. There are those political pundits in town who have long advocated the random selection of names from the Boston telephone directory as a more satisfactory method of choosing members of the City Council and School Committee, and Mayor '77 could be a big step toward such a plan. Perhaps the new lottery will eventually diversify, as The Game has done, and chances on these positions could be sold for, say, twenty-five cents—on an at-large basis, of course.

But let's not get carried away. It's enough that someone at City Hall has had the hindsight to know what 1976 meant to the Hub, and the foresight to know what the city needs in 1977. Mayor '77 is only the beginning, but it's a lot better than sitting around waiting for the Tricentennial.

35

My Wood's in Early This Year

WELL, I'VE got my wood in. To most of you, that doesn't sound like much of an accomplishment, I'm certain. But if you had been a member of our household any autumn during the past decade, you would understand why I'm proud enough of the achievement to go public with the news. I have to do at least this much to make sure that I am convinced this is not a dream, that I won't awaken and find the barn and the woodshed still gapingly empty of firewood, the way they have been ever since we built the place.

There was a time when I said, "We'll get all the wood we need off the beach," up in the coves where the September storms pile great haystacks of silver, salt-soaked driftwood. I had visions that living by the sea could also mean living from the sea. I soon found that no amount of badgering could get the boys out on cold November weekend afternoons to wrestle with the tangled leviathan logs. I was left to bring in what I could carry, and the stove soon consumed that.

Then would come the moment that every local woodcutter waits for: the late, plaintive November phone call—"Have you got any stovewood left?" That inquiry is the absolute proof that the wood-cutter has hooked a sucker, a grasshopper of a provider who fancies that somehow he will survive, that summer is for playing, and to hell with the ants who work through July and August piling architect's drawings of woodpiles, each designed like an oak Taj Mahal, lattice monuments to thrift, diligence, foresight, planning and industry. Now the grasshopper faces his fate, the playboy's penalty. "Well," comes the barely restrained joyous voice over the phone, "I don't know as I do. We're about delivered out of wood for this season. Most folks ordered their's some time ago, don't you know." Pause for effect. "But I might be able to scrape up a cord or two. I'll see what I can do."

There is a vacuum of communication after that hint that help may be on its way. I am just too frightened to ask the price, frightened because I know that I have been skewered once more by my own procrastination. But eventually I do ask, and the inevitable penalty slams my wallet with the finality of a guillotine's blade. As my deficit rolls into the basket, I tell myself for the umpteenth time that this tragedy will not happen next year.

Well, this year it hasn't. I have my wood in. Can you believe it? I begin to wonder if I am threatened by maturity. Do those cords of oak and maple stacked in the woodshed (they must, of course, still be cut and split) indicate a dehydration of the juices of impracticality that have flowed so relentlessly through my being? Am I, at long last, responding to the pleadings of my parents, pleas for responsible behavior issued so many decades ago?

I'm not certain of the reasons, but I am not too worried about any dulling of my impulsive edge. Only I know why I have my wood in. It was a golden September morning, still summery enough to allow contemplation of an afternoon sail on silken waters. I was driving to the office (the place where the children have been told I work) when my accustomed progress was slowed by an elderly, red pick-up truck. As I downshifted and passed with my usual Grand Prix elan, I noticed the sign "Firewood For Sale" on the truck's door. Pulling over, I gestured to the somewhat astonished driver, and he rather gingerly also pulled over, waiting in the cab to see what wreckage fate had cast on his shore this lovely September day.

Without allowing myself a moment to hesitate, I ordered up the cords, quite heedless then of where I would acquire the wherewithal for payment on delivery day. But the pick-up driver was not a fellow to look a gift order in the mouth, and within forty-eight hours there was a confusion of wood dumped in our driveway and a burly fellow at the doorway asking for a check.

That's how I got my wood in, and I'm still proud. Indeed, the more I read about inflation, the more I realize that we grasshoppers may be the most unwitting success stories ever written. "Be self-employed" say the instructions on how to beat inflation (who would hire a grasshopper?), "Be a borrower . . ." Oh boy, do I follow that advice. "Have a large mortgage . . ." What is more tangible than oak and maple? I declare, everything I was once told was wrong I am now told is right. Which makes me wonder: was I wrong to get the wood in so early?

CITYSIDE / TRENDS

Calculating Your Urban Chic

BEING A terribly sophisticated observer, you have undoubtedly noted the recent passing of rural chic. And good riddance, you might add. The only problem now, of course, is what you do with your L.L. Bean chino pants and your memories of John Lincoln Wright and the Sour Mash Boys. Might as well toss them into your Jotul woodstove.

In the meantime, *urban* chic stands ready to be embraced. This is the hot phenomenon of the late 1970s, fueled by talk of the "back to the city movement." But before you sell your log home near Brattleboro and move into a Victorian house in Jamaica Plain (which is about to become the trendy place to live in Boston, replacing such bygone pacesetters as the South End, the North End, and Charlestown), you would be wise to see if you qualify.

To guard against impostors, a team of local researchers has developed the following socio-economic examination. In order to test your level of urban chic, simply award yourself the number of points indicated.

Five points for each of the following owned: 1. a brass bed; 2. a folding Plexiglas chair imported from Italy; 3. a Kovacs floor lamp.

Five points for each of the following you are planning to own within thirty days: 1. a ten-speed French bicycle; 2. a walnut toilet seat; 3. a used pinball machine.

Fifteen points if you have ever witnessed either: 1. Kevin White shopping at DeLuca's Market; 2. Martin Slobodkin coming home from a party; 3. a piece of glass falling from the John Hancock Tower.

Ten points for each of the following you have patronized within that last thirty days: 1. Brookstone; 2. the Cafe Plaza; 3. any used-clothing store in the South End.

Five points for each of the following served at your most recent dinner party: 1. Fauchon condiments from Bloomingdale's; 2. meat from Brigham Provision Co.; 3. anything from Malben's.

Ten points for partaking of any of the following within the past fortnight: 1. brunch at Parker's; 2. lunch at the Premier Deli; 3. dinner at the Houndstooth; 4. dancing at Boston Boston.

Ten points for installing any of the following in your home within the past year: 1. track lighting; 2. a ceiling fan; 3. a skylight; 4. a portable greenhouse.

Five points for attending any of the following since New Year's Day: 1. a midnight movie; 2. a matinee theater performance; 3. a concert by Willie "Loco" Alexander and the Boom-Boom Band.

Now take five points *away* if you can claim any of the following: 1. owning an automobile built since 1971; 2. still believing the bleachers at Fenway Park are a nice place to be; 3. regularly visiting Faneuil Hall Marketplace.

Now add up your points. If you scored 100 or more, you are clearly riddled through and through with urban chic and are hereby declared a person for the '70s. If not, kindly leave town as soon as possible—preferably aboard the nearest John Deere tractor.

Memorial Day

I SUPPOSE I have known ever since I was a child what Memorial Day is for. When I was growing up, it was called Decoration Day, and among the rituals required was the placing of flowers on the graves of soldiers who had fought in the nation's wars. The name of the day has been changed, but the apparent traditions have not: Memorial Day is still a time for honoring the war dead with speeches, ceremonies, parades, and—for some—visits to cemeteries with flowers in hand.

As a veteran (WW II) and an observer of Memorial Days for more than five decades, I approached last Monday's holiday with the same ambivalence I have ever since 1945 and my release from military obligations. I have difficulty rationalizing my reluctance to openly join the parades and expressions of honor; instead of putting on a uniform several sizes too small and marching down Maine Street with the Boy Scouts—as several of my acquaintances and contemporaries do—I would much rather brace myself against such sentiments and, instead, revel in the natural wonders this last week in May traditionally bestows on the Maine countryside.

There is no other week in Maine when the abundance of the season is so vividly in evidence. No matter what the weather conditions—and, over the years, these have covered quite a range—nature will not be stopped from saying: "This is my finest hour." On many Memorial Day mornings, I have smelled the fragrance of a thousand lilac blossoms as the breeze off the water carries it through the open kitchen window. Poppies, apple blossoms, daisies, violets, and the full, green foliage of the elms, oaks, maples, birch and willow . . . the entire floral and arboreal cast of thousands that so illuminates our fields and forests is at its absolute peak. On some Memorial Day mornings it has seemed to me that this blossoming and blooming world is on the brink of exploding with its own sweetness, as if one more day of such beauty would be unbearable.

Part of this, I know, has to do with the length of the winters, the hesitancy of April, and early May's false starts. These are climatic truths in this part of the world that do not necessarily apply to other regions. In Washington, for example, the lilacs have already bloomed, and long ago faded. So it is the Yankee in me that speaks of Memorial Day memories. It is because, like all of you, I have waited so long for the evidence of summer that this day has become more of a celebration of life than an honoring of death.

In a way, I suppose, that's what has bothered me over the years. Every Memorial Day finds me struggling with a bit of guilt at feeling so overjoyed at the season's extravagant display instead of being consumed with a kind of quiet sorrow for the thousands of brave young veterans who have long since gone to their early and honorable graves. I think about the men in my squadron who did not come home with me, and I wonder to myself if they would want me to be marching along Maine Street or giving some sort of predictable speech in the town square, all in the name of their fine memory.

I decide they would not. I decide that the day is a way of making life easier for the living, for those who did not go to war. It eases their anguish a bit to tell themselves they, at the very least, have set aside a bit of time to recognize that the war dead do exist, that once there were brave men who gave their lives for this, or that, noble purpose. I can cop out a bit, because I was a boy with those boys, and I know that most of us didn't know much about what we were doing, or why. "We're here because we're here . . ." is the way the song used to go that we sang while we marched, and it's a true song.

So I resolve my ambivalence by going to the simplest ceremony in the smallest Maine village nearby—a place where I can smell the lilacs, hear the river rushing, and watch the oriole fly by as I listen to the speeches and the prayers. That way, the holiday does not go unobserved, but becomes, for me, more a celebration of life than an honoring of death.

41

A Long-Running Show with a Cast of Thousands

ONCE UPON a time, all you had to worry about on the streets of Boston were maniacal drivers, belligerent panhandlers and an overabundance of *excrementun canis*. That was before jogging, of course. In the likelihood you have been traveling through deepest Swaziland for the past few years, I should point out that jogging has recently become a certified urban trend. It is now more popular in Boston than either jaywalking or declaring for public office. There are so many runners on the local highways and byways that the pedestrian who passes through life at a walk risks having his body covered with Adidas tracks. Jogging is so trendy in Boston that a television movie, called "See How She Runs," was made about it. It starred Joanne Woodward and a cast of trotting thousands.

I have a friend who claims to run through the city at all hours of the day and night. He contends that such adventures are perfectly safe because muggers 1) don't like moving targets and 2) know that joggers don't usually carry large wads of cash in their sweat pants. Street crime has its own version of the arms race, however. A young man who was recently charged with attacking two females joggers on the Esplanade was allegedly using a Moped to catch his victims.

In any case, such assaults will not dissuade the confirmed urban runner, who knows just how well his environment is suited to his sport. Basketball players need hoops, skiers need mountains, tennis players need courts. Awash amidst the emotional instant replay of the ME generation, however, the jogger requires only his own body and a reasonably clear piece of the planet. The city will do just fine.

Of course, running still needs a few additives before it will qualify as a household word—an authentic superstar, for instance, and some sort of elaborate TV Event akin to the Bobby Riggs vs. Billie Jean King tennis extravaganza of 1973. Nevertheless, it is the first trend sport that hasn't been basically a suburban item, as were golf, skiing and tennis in their days of complete ultrachic.

Which means that the sport is likely to grow in the city. I have nightmares of walking out of my home some morning and finding the street an exact replica of Hopkinton at high noon on Patriots Day. Even worse, I'm beginning to feel thoroughly out of touch at social gatherings, a discontent due primarily to my inability to converse for hours about oxygen exchange rates.

(I used to jog, by the way. I did it a few years ago for about four months, after which time I felt no better or worse than before I started. It was Bruce Springsteen who was born to run, not I.)

Nothing seems capable of discouraging the citified jogger. Winter's snowstorms only cause him to toss another towel around his neck. Weaving among automobile drivers who haven't the slightest interest in his welfare only fires his calves. How long will it be before Boston—as New York did recently in the Empire State Building—stages a foot race up the stairwell of the John Hancock Tower?

My friend who runs at all hours tells me that jogging dating bars are strictly passe, which indicates to him that the trend may be peaking in the city. I doubt it. Just the other day I noticed someone jogging through Faneuil Hall Marketplace in pleated pants and a "Boogie While You Run" T-shirt. If it has come to that, the album of the sound track of the movie of the book can't be far behind.

What's a Calendar for, Anyway?

THIS YEAR'S calendars are well on their way to losing their temporal effectiveness. Replacements to take their place, however, are everywhere in evidence. My insurance agent keeps me well supplied; I suppose I could have a dozen of his "rural scene" calendars if I asked. It's a matter of functional generosity: the presence of these colorful chronometrics bearing his name not only keep me informed of the date but also remind me when premiums are due.

I am much more partial to the one calendar we keep by the stove at home. It tells me the tides, the phases of the moon, the time of sunset and sunrise; and, as the pages turn, imparts bits and pieces of the lore of ancient mariners, italicized in almanac form beneath a series of fine pen-and-ink nautical illustrations.

There is one problem. Over the past several years, various family members have taken to jotting notations and observations in the white space left by each day in the calendar's design. I'm reasonably certain the space was left there by the calendar creator as a spot for listing appointments, birthdays, and the other temporal paraphernalia of our lives. In our house, that function has been largely ignored. Instead, the entries are notes pertaining to the natural events that take place beyond our windows.

A day in May, for example, will be annotated thus: "Saw the first terns today . . . two of them went by the cove . . ." Or: "GBH fishing by the point for the first time since January . . ." Those initials—GBH—stand for Great Blue Heron—more particularly the patriarch that has claimed the cove near our place as his very own, to be defended against all comers.

What has happened over the years since these seasonal, natural events have been tracked by our household observers is that no one wants to scrap such valuable information. You can understand. It's perfectly OK, desirable, in fact, to toss out a calendar full of such passé data as: "Sam, dentist, 10 A.M.," or "car due for oil change," or even "Sam late for school, again!." Like so much of the year gone by, those minutiae of life are not only part of the past; they are eminently forgottable and quite routine. The car will need another oil change in the year ahead, and Sam will surely be late for school "again!"

What is not forgettable and not routine is the date of the terns return, the first ice on the bay, or, even more momentous, the actual day, hour, and weather conditions when the ice began to break up and go groaning down the channel. These, and similar sorts of data—first frost, first crocus, first ripe tomato, first quart of homegrown strawberries—are more than mere notes on the passage of time; they are a gardener's guide, a weather watcher's yardstick, a signal that hope is permissible, an irrefutable document stating that spring will arrive, summer will bloom and the leaves of autumn will tumble.

A country person needs reassurance, sometimes, that this cycle will continue. And, to ease whatever doubts may sprout from the dormant seeds of anxiety we all keep within us, a country person needs to know just what day, last year, and the year before, the ice began to turn from white to gray, and when the first long fissure that appeared one warm March afternoon would fracture at last, revealing a vein of blue water sparkling in the brilliant sun: the essence of spring—fluid, bright, surprising.

We need to know these things and so we have saved the calendars of the past several years. They do not get scrapped with last year's phone books, nor with the "rural scene" insurance agent's gift, but they are piled there on a corner of the kitchen counter like the record of a king's reign etched in the walls of his tomb. Thumbing through them, I can tell you quite precisely when to begin to look for GBH, or when to wish him farewell. I can also document the destruction of the dock in a January gale, or pinpoint the moment of the season's first measurable snowfall.

Our natural library grows, year by year, a swelling testimony to the wonder of living in Maine, one of the few places where the seasons march with such majesty and presence that their procession, year after year, is a pageant to be researched and observed with constant wonder, eternal gratitude, and calendars from the past.

Swaps Might Help

NEW YORK. Cities are like people, the theory goes. No two are alike. New York and Boston have about as much in common as Andy Warhol and Louise Day Hicks. Still, you'll find no knocking of New York here, no searching for the worm in the Big Apple. I *like* New York, which puts me among a total of precisely seven Americans, the other six of whom are viewed by their neighbors as being the social equals of Caryl Chessman.

As I write this, the man on television—who looks disturbingly like Tom Ellis or Chuck Scarborough—has just announced that the temperature is no less than "96 degrees in midtown Manhattan." Down here on the Lower East Side, there are rumblings that the citizenry is about to take over all the boarded-up buildings. Up in the East 80s, people are so hot they're fanning themselves with their jewelry. Why couldn't I have taken a pleasant weekend in the country instead of choosing to melt to death?

Nevertheless, the foray into Gotham has once again been educational. Boston could learn a few things from New York. And, likewise, the Apple from the Hub. In fact, if the two cities could work out the following four-for-four swap, involving no cash or draft choices . . . well, the trade would help both teams, as they say.

From New York, Boston would receive:

1. Public Transportation. Its personnel are as uncivil as those lovable MBTA types and its subway trains look like rejected album covers for Big Brother and the Holding Company, but at least New York's public transportation system is predicated on the belief that you can, indeed, get people there from here. In Boston, the term "public transportation" is considered a contradiction of terms.

2. Life After Midnight. The Hub operates under a variation of the Cinderella tale, to wit: Everybody who isn't home by the time the clock strikes twelve is some kind of fruit. In New York, you can get anything you want at 4 A.M., including bagels and the mumps.

3. Firsts and Onlys. Two evenings ago I saw the final showing of a film in Manhattan, and it hasn't even opened yet in Boston. Last night I saw a British comedy revue which won't get any closer to the Hub than a trip across the Triborough Bridge. Except for pre-Broadway theater runs, Boston seems to get most entertainment eleven months after New York, if at all.

4. The Melting Pot Theory. In New York, every bus ride looks like a meeting of the UN General Assembly. Maybe it's the "We're-all-in-this-together" notion, but New Yorkers seem to be able to tolerate their ethnic differences better than people in Boston. Of course, maybe it's because they can't understand each other.

In return, New York would receive from Boston:

1. Cleaner air. Imagine the Callahan Tunnel with its lights out, and you have a pretty good idea of New York at noon on a sunny day. If King Kong and Fay Wray were still having an affair at the top of the Empire State Building, no one on the ground would know.

2. Smoother streets. Cross my heart on a stack of Bibles, honest to God: New York's streets make Boston's look like the tops of billiard tables. Yesterday a bus going on First Avenue hit a pothole and disappeared from sight. Rescue patrols were sent in, and *they* disappeared, too.

3. Fenway Park. Once upon a time, out in the Bronx, lived

Yankee Stadium. It was truly magnificent and was called "The House That Ruth Built." Now it has been "rebuilt" (with public money!) into a modern concrete edifice which looks as if it belongs in some place like Cincinnati or San Diego. It should be called "The House That George Steinbrenner Built."

4. A Handle. Boston is a city you can get a grip on. Which is another way of saying it has definition. (Or "livability," as people such as Kevin White like to put it, in apparent contrast to "deathability.") New York, on the other hand, is an amorphous and teeming mass which always seems to be on the brink of Armageddon. It is as easy to comprehend as a Jackson Pollock painting turned sideways.

To consummate this trade, representatives of both cities could meet in a neutral site to sign the necessary papers. Let's say Bridgeport, Conn. That should make them appreciate what they're getting.

COUNTRYSIDE / TRENDS

Ode to an Oak

IT WAS spring four years ago when we built the dirt road that winds through the woods to our home. The land we chose had been farmed forty years before; there had been meadows and fences where we found pine and birch. Some had to be cut to make room for the slim road that would lead to the site of our new home, but there were not the forests primeval that had once been cleared by the former homesteaders of this small Maine point. Shipbuilders had been the first to harvest those huge trees. They felled them from the water's edge back and kept cutting until they had taken most of the wood and fashioned it into the sloops and schooners that sailed from the cove to the Barbados and the China Sea.

After the shipbuilders had done their work, farmers arrived to plow the forests cleared in the name of commerce. Hayfields and cornfields spread slowly as men and oxen worked to loosen the mighty stumps left by the shipbuilders.

Then the grandchildren of those farmers moved into town, became shopkeepers, school teachers, doctors and engineers. As they did, the forests began to reclaim the farms.

That's when we arrived. Because it was spring, our schoolboy sons and their friends were eager to work in the young woods. We plotted the path of the road along an old carriage trail, we curved and bent the course so it would avoid as many trees as possible. The sharpest curve was plotted so it would spare the huge line of oaks that marched in single file above the pines and birches.

Those oaks had been young seedlings when the shipbuilders had swung their axes; when the farmers arrived, one line of the trees was left—an immortal marker stretching due north and south to separate the fields of one neighbor from another. Our road crossed part of that line; we bent it so it would fit between two trees; neither of the giants had to come down.

But last year, one of the roadside oaks had died. No green leaves pushed from its branches; the tree just stood there, its bare, gray limbs spread stark against the summer sky. The road must have come too close. Perhaps the pressure of the passing cars had crushed too many roots. Whatever unseen injury had occurred, it had proven a mortal wound. The great line tree we had worked so hard to save had given up the ghost.

It stood there a year, indomitable, towering and awesome. I knew it would have to be cut down, but I could not bring myself to swing the axe. This fall on a bright Saturday, impulsively, I took two of the same sons who had helped build the road and we went to fell the tree. I rationalized that the approaching winter storms could drop it on the road, perhaps blocking the way when it was needed most. Also, the giant held a month's supply of stove wood in its trunks and limbs—wood we needed to help us keep warm.

The two-man saw cut deep; the seasoned wood snapped clean

and the tree came down with a crash that was heard a mile away on that autumn afternoon. The ground shook; the three of us trembled at the shattering consequences of our deed.

On the ground, the oak looked even larger than it had standing. It took a while to walk the distance from the trunk to the tip of the furthest branches. Working like pygmies over an elephant's carcass, the three of us sawed and hacked and pulled and heaved for the rest of that day and most of the next to get the bones of the fallen giant cut into sections small enough for us to move. Then we piled them atop each other like a temple in front of the barn where they wait to be sawn still more and split, stacked and carried to the stoves inside the house.

I counted 120 rings on the stump. Ten years before the Civil War, the tree had been taller than most men. It had gotten its start just after the shipbuilders had left this land for the lure of California gold, and it had lived a proud life as the guardian of a pact between neighbors.

How much better are old oaks than old men. Oaks grow stronger and mightier as they grow older. Their years push them toward the sky instead of bending them against their frailties and fading senses. The longer an oak lives, the more lordly it becomes; a man who lives too long can know no pride.

An old man passes with a whisper; he slips almost silently. The crashing of an oak trembles an entire afternoon. The service an oak performs reaches its peak with every year it lives; centuries only add to the measure of an oak's performance. Men become infants once again, helpless with the weight of their years.

And after death the bones of an oak bring light, warmth and structure to the world while the carcass of a man becomes a matter for disposal.

Yet it is man who brings down the oaks. For that, it seems, we pay a heavy price.

50

Lifestyles

Spring to the Ear

SPRING, BELIEVE it or not, is scheduled to arrive officially just a few minutes after midnight twelve days from now. Searching for signs of the season in this northeastern corner of the nation has always been a quixotic mission; looking for them in the middle of the night could be called downright foolish.

Nevertheless, the equinoctial moment will be marked, and all of us will be treated to news of pussy willows, croci in bloom, and the traditional photographs of skunk cabbage unfurling in the marsh. For many observers of this most eagerly awaited season, spring is a visual event. It's what a person can see, so the conventional wisdom goes, that verifies celestial movements the calendar has already documented. Straw boaters, Easter bunnies, greening willows, departing ice, and the return of motorcycle police are some of the more familiar indicators that New England is about to be resuscitated.

"Signs of spring," they are called, and more power to them. For me, however, spring has always been more aural than visual; it is the sounds of the season that have become my most certain reassurance that March is not some dirty trick played to test our Yankee endurance. As the vernal equinox approaches, I listen more intently than I look. Sometimes the sounds come to me as a surprise, carried on the softer winds of the season, and this has its advantages over visual evidence: that has to be searched out; the spring music that reaches my ears often comes on its own, making its own particular announcement.

I have, for example, lain in my night-time bed, the chamber window open more than it has been since November, and listened to a natural barrage that occurs only every now and then, but always—when it does—during March. In the darkness I hear a deep, ponderous groaning, a giant sighing and rumbling in the distance. It is followed by concussive thuds; they seem to shake the house as distant cannon might. There is no rhythm to the rumpus; the groans and thuds are random, closer one minute, then silent.

What I am hearing is the bay ice breaking on the crest of a midnight tide and a warm wind from the south. A winter's work is being undone, a monument to January is being demolished. As the tide swells beneath the tugging of a waxing moon, it cracks seams in salt ice already made vulnerable by the day's warming sun. Some circumstantial convection of forces I have yet to understand sets the entire bay to shattering, and the night is filled with the thunder of the crush. It is a rare and awesome sound, this surrender of the ice, and for me it is a more certain signal of the season than any greening of the willows.

And when the ice has gone, its cracked pieces swept clean by the tide's swift broom, another almost forgotten sound comes to keep us company at breakfast. It is the cacaphony of the sea gulls, talking, screaming, complaining, bickering, celebrating and generally enjoying the process of filling the morning air with the sound of their first assembly on the mud flats since December when the flats were stilled under their icy shield. Sometimes I

54

think the gulls know more about when the ice will leave than any weather expert. I see them days before ice-out, gliding in the distance, waiting, gathering.

Then, when the flats are bare and vulnerable, littered with the ice-battered flotsam of an entire winter, the gulls come in droves to pick over the bones of the cold. It matters not if our every door and window is closed against a March gale, the sound of 300 sea-gulls screaming can be heard. It is a shrill guarantee of restoration and rebirth; it is another certain signal.

When the tide floods the flats and the gulls are floated from their feeding, eiders and old-squaws flock to the bay; unlike the sea gulls, these waterfowl must have diving space to feed. As they collect in ever growing numbers over the mussel bars, their melodious calling ripples in with the breeze. Theirs is a warbling, mysterious gabble—musical, pitched high, like a flute, much more gentle than the gull sounds. It, too, bespeaks spring. In a few weeks, the flocks that gather will be fractured into nesting pairs. Then the true renewal will begin.

That time is a while off yet; but it is not too early now for us to begin to listen.

CITYSIDE / LIFESTYLES

It All May Be Worth a Quarter

RECENTLY I read an amusing account of what we now call "panhandling," which is a euphemism left over from the 1960s that allows us to romanticize the act of begging in the streets. This particular magazine article, reversed the queen-for-a-day theme, and I was thus given entry into the mind of an instant down-and-outer. All well and good, but if the beggar can produce such a primer, what about the beggee (one from whom money is

55

begged)? Certainly he or she could use a few weapons in waging the continual urban skirmish for the quarter.

You can, of course, always say no to panhandlers, but such a response is utterly lacking in style. The best of them are totally amusing and the worst merely a nuisance, and their Boylston street hustles are favors which should be returned in kind. No, "No" will simply never do, even if that is what you meant to say all along. Imagination is needed.

My favorite beggee is a friend who considers himself a budding magician. He reacts to a panhandler's pitch by "finding" a coin behind the startled mendicant's ear. The reaction to such a ploy usually depends on the sobriety of the victim—it is not unusual for the more inebriated to frantically rub their hair in search of additional coins. Cruel? Perhaps, but hardly in the same class as heating a quarter in an automobile cigarette lighter and then dropping it from a gloved fist into a bare hand.

For beggees with less talent than a magician and more sensitivity than a sadist, the following may be of help in future confrontations throughout downtown Boston:

1. Keep one pocket empty at all times, ready to be pulled inside out as proof of shared poverty. The ringing of change in other pockets can be muffled by wads of Kleenex.

2. On occasion, get the jump on an approaching panhandler by asking for *his* spare change before he has an opportunity to speak.

3. React to a hustle by muttering in a foreign language. "Je ne parle pas Anglais" will do just fine. If you don't know a foreign language, make one up.

4. If possible, outhustle the hustler. Invent a story even more outrageous than his own, sprinkled with pious references to your family. For example, explain that you can't contribute to his bus ticket to New York because you're saving money to attend your mother's funeral in Bogota.

5. Since appearances count, try to outfunk the panhandler. Wear absolutely no cashmere or suede. Don't try to sneak by with prewashed jeans. Stick to basic tattered levis and a turned up collar. Slouch a lot and, if at all possible, carry a bottle of club soda in a rumpled paper bag.

6. Practice and perfect the fast shuffle. This includes spotting a panhandler from a distance of at least one block, accelerating quickly, and brushing past with a perfunctory "I'm late." The fast shuffle is not the same as crossing the street to avoid confrontation, which is the approximate equal of saying no.

7. Tell the panhandler you'll be happy to help him out, but only if he takes American Express. Either that, or explain that you need a receipt for cash.

8. Say you gave at the office.

If none of these devices work, your panhandler has earned his money. Besides, the panhandling ritual remains a part of life in Boston, and one that does no more to foul the air than does the nearest pigeon or politician. Now that's worth a quarter.

COUNTRYSIDE / LIFESTYLES

Gulls

I CAN HEAR the gulls every day now, not just occasionally when one happens to fly over the house, or the wind is right. That was the way it was in the winter when the bay was frozen and its icy fortress covered the mud flats with foot-thick walls of congealed brine. That slab of ice stretched miles from the shore, as far as I could see, too far for the voices of the gulls to carry. They could find no life on that barren moonscape of bay ice; they survived the winter in places beyond my ken—places where open water and winter fishermen provided them with enough food to keep them from starving.

But the living is easier now that we are past May's green brink. The ice has long since vanished, the mud flats are exposed at every ebb tide, the gulls gather in their raucous flocks, and in the cacophony of their coarse voices I hear a wonderful song of summer. It is so ordinary, so much a part of every day and night that it is taken for granted, becomes as unacknowledged as the rising sun or the leafing trees. Yet, every so often, I hear one gull cry and I stop long enough to realize how much I missed that silly sound when winter kept it silenced.

I say "gulls" with the kind of carelessness an ornithologist would condemn; the term is a general one covering an entire family of birds. To be more specific, I should say herring gull, and talk about the most common, large, white bird that inhabits the New England coast, and most of the rest of the coastal regions of the nation. Along this Maine shore, there are also great blackback gulls, laughing gulls, bonaparte's gulls, ringbill gulls, and the graceful terns with their higher, more haunting calls.

I know them all, but none as well as the common herring gull. That bird, it seems to me, has been with me ever since my earliest memories of summers on the beach as an infant who was tossed into the sea to learn to swim before I learned to walk. I watched the gulls then, and on into boyhood. I learned to count on them as fish finders when I became a commercial fisherman, and, as my life unfolded, I came to realize that I would never live for very long in any place so far from the water that gulls seldom visited.

I have held herring gulls in my hands. Up close, they are definitely not your idea of a graceful creature. They are mean, they tried to bite and peck even as I struggled to free them from the fishing line they had stupidly entangled themselves in, and they stink of the fishy foods they like best. Having looked deep into them, I can tell you that gull's eyes are cold, yellow, and full of fierceness. But freed from the snare, tossed into the air, the bird becomes a gliding presence, capturing the essence of flight so purely that it becomes the symbol of all our longings for freedom.

I don't think of the gull's fierce eyes of cold yellow when one swoops over the house as I step outdoors to greet the warm, May sun. Nor do I recall the rankness of the fish stink when I watch a herring gull glide across the water as easily as a dandelion seed in the wind. What I remember is how often I have seen the sight, and how wondrous it always is. It is a kind of poetry, a verse written on a sea breeze, a stanza that would be much more highly valued if only it were not so common.

I can recall being in the narrow streets of the heart of waterfront cities like Portland and Boston when I heard a herring gull's high, hoarse call. Looking up, I could see the bird, winging across the rooftops as easily as it could bank between the peaks of two waves. Then I would say to myself, this city has got to be liveable, the gulls are here in the center of downtown. It is when I get to places where the gulls have never been that I sense the need to leave.

Now that spring is truly here, the voices of the gulls never stop. They tumble in across the bay through my days and nights, and in the risings and fallings of the shrill, irreverent calls, I hear the voices of my past, the sounds of my own childhood, the songs of my days on the water, and the poetry of nights on the coast. These rude and common birds bring me this, and for that I am always grateful when the mudflats warm and the gulls come back again.

CITYSIDE / LIFESTYLES

The Street of Cheek and Chic

I TOOK A long walk along Boylston street the other day, and I'm here to tell you it's still champ. No doubt about it. I knew the other pretenders to the title of Boston's Main Street were in trouble when the wino approached me in front of Lord and Taylor and asked me for a quarter because his Bristol Myers stock was down. That's not only an original gaff, but maybe even a true one. I checked, and Bristol Myers was down two points.

But that's Boylston street for you. A year ago I spent more time than I thought humanly possible on that 2.2 miles of high and low life, and wrote a long magazine story which concluded that the avenue is Boston's most definitive thoroughfare. I still go there a lot because it conjures up all the ambivalence I feel toward the city. In fact, I think all persons contemplating a move into what we now refer to as the "inner city" ought to be made to walk along Boylston from Massachusetts avenue to Park Square. If they find the sights too extreme, they would probably be better off staying in Braintree or Waltham or Wakefield.

It's absolutely crazy, this mix of Big Macs and Chateaubriand. No wonder it was named after Dr. Zabdiel Boylston, whom the early nineteenth-century townsfolk couldn't decide whether to honor or hang after he performed the first inoculations for smallpox. The street was historically a buffer zone between the beau monde of Back Bay and hoi polloi to the south, but replacing thirty acres of railroad yards with the Prudential Center changed all that in 1965. Since then the street has been an everyman's land of chic and cheek. Hookers and street vendors ply their trades on equal social footing with matrons and stockbrokers, each group ignoring the other with a kind of blissful mutual consent.

Technically, Boylston street begins at the King of Pizza in the Combat Zone and ends at Leahy's Exxon at the corner of Brookline avenue. In between can be found the Institute of Contemporary Art, Burger King, the Tennis and Racquet Club, the Pru Cinema, the Boston Public Library, the Fatted Calf, Saks Fifth Avenue, McDonald's, the Copley Plaza Hotel, the Bulkie, IBM, Waterrest, and Shreve, Crump and Low. In fact, there's nothing you can't get on Boylston street, provided you have the money. And even if you don't, panhandling is as accepted as an American Express card.

The architecture, of course, is an abysmal failure. The street looks like the creation of a paint-by-the-numbers artist who got confused. Buildings are hopelessly mismatched, and all but a few of the once-stately nineteenth-century town houses have been obliterated by storefronts with pancake make-up. Sign control now exists, but that is a bit like opening a bank account after the burglar has found all your money under the mattress. The retail turnover is tremendous, with a Brigham's seemingly always coming and a Senor Pizza always going.

Still, to criticize Boylston street for not being planned is to miss its point. It is a frontier street, complete with saloons, an opera house, and its own brand of law and order. It doesn't try; it just *is*. Pre-Algonquin Indians were fishing on what is now Boylston street more than 4000 years ago, and today the chanting Hare Krishna movement wants to catch a few converts on broad sidewalks. You can walk into the Dunkin' Donuts shop between Exeter and Fairfield streets and view a counter-full of coffee-gulping characters who look capable of committing any act at any moment. Or you can wander into the Public Library and take a seat across from an elderly citizen who gives few outward signs of human life. Chances are that if you find yourself on Boylston street you probably belong there. Almost everyone does. And is.

COUNTRYSIDE / LIFESTYLES

Due-Bill Days

THESE ARE what I call my due-bill days. Perhaps you are unfamiliar with the term. It's newspaper talk and, for all I know, may be restricted to this particular trade. A due-bill is what develops when, for example, the Parker House advertises in an out-of-town publication. However, instead of paying cash for the transaction, the hotel begins to bank the equivalent credit on its books. Then, whenever the publisher or some fortunate reporter gets asked to Boston for a meeting or a convention, the cost of the night's lodging is deducted from the due-bill.

I don't have any such due-bills at any Boston hostelries, not even the Parker House, nor have I enjoyed any such barter in the past. But I like the term, even though I heard it used for years before I understood what it signifies.

I like it especially on these softest of the new summer days. And whenever there is an especially vibrant morning, alive with fresh dew and a brilliant sunrise—a prelude to a day that I know from the start is going to be a superlative in this season's lexicon—then I make it a due-bill day. I trade it for the credits I have amassed in November, December, January and on through April, and even May.

I try to start at the beginning. On days like this in late June, I will usually have worked my way through mid-December. In my memory, I am standing on my roof, shovel in hand with my legs planted in snow up to my waist. My heart thumps with the exertion of trying to move the stuff off the relatively flat top of our home, our shelter and one of the bank's most top-heavy mortgages. First, we had a twelve-inch snow storm, then another fourteen, then more, and now this downpour of December rain. It is soaking the snow, saturating my drifted roof with a massive, soggy burden that may be too heavy for our beams to bear. All day the news reports of collapsed buildings have been erupting from the radio and my anxieties just can't take it any more.

So here I am, aloft in the deepening dusk, standing like a sailor atop a storm-tossed ship while the wind beats at my ears and the torrents soak my clothes. This is the way heart attacks are encouraged, I tell myself as I struggle with the incredibly heavy and stubborn mass that the once-fluffy snow has become. Soon, it is dark, the rain is starting to freeze and the entire mess of wetness is congealing into an incredible, glacial mass. But more than half the roof has been cleared, thanks to the grudging help of two sons who are convinced of my insanity. I stagger into the house—now dark and chilly from a town-wide power failure—and light fires and candles before I strip off my chill, soaked clothing. Meanwhile, the rain has turned to snow again, the wind is howling from the nor'west and I look out the window as a supplicant, begging to be spared more such elemental punishment.

62

This day in June may be valued at half that day in December. If two such due-bill days come back to back, then I will trade away the total episode of rooftop suffering. A full week of late June delights will move me through the days of irritation caused when January's freakish cold and frozen snow kept the drive from being plowed and had me walking a mile or so in below-zero discomfort.

It is thus that I spend these mid-summer weeks, reveling in June's unabashed luxury, but, at the same time, keeping my seasonal books in order, checking my due-bill days one by one until the entire Maine winter and haphazard spring has been discharged. In a good summer, I can pull even as early as mid-August. Then, with all obligations cleared, come the bonus days which are so prized in this corner of the northeast.

The last two weeks in August, all of September and most of October arrive without liens, untrammeled by winter's due-bills. They are the gift we Yankees share in good conscience, knowing that it was during these sweet moments of June and July that we balanced the books with December and January.

CITYSIDE / LIFESTYLES

An UnCommon Place

"TOM THE Oneman Band," who is doing brisk business these days outside the Park Street subway station by providing a musical interlude while wishing passersby "a long, healthy and happy life" via his sandwich board, undoubtedly realizes he could never cut it down the road at the Public Garden. A completely different clientele, for one thing. For another, the local constabulary would strip him of his drum and tambourine before he got eight bars into his opening number.

So Tom the Oneman Band works the edge of Boston Common, that forty-five-acre chunk of turf and humanity which is so utterly, completely, wonderfully . . . common. Beats me how tourists are always getting it confused with the Garden, which is a bit like mistaking the Starlite Motel for the Ritz Carlton.

Even before the Garden's latest facelift—which is progressing with all the dispatch of the Hundred Years' War—it was a more elegant younger sister of the Common mall. Why, there are even 25,000 imported bees living peacefully in a log on an island in the Garden's lagoon.

So while the Garden is a relatively polite oasis of willows, flower beds, Swan Boats and elderly women reading *Guideposts* magazine, the Common is Boston's own little version of the wild west. Grease up the ten-speed, let out the doberman, roll the joints for retail, tune the guitar and flex the wrist for Frisbee season. Everything apparently is legal here, even if it involves surpassing the speed of sound while riding a skateboard.

Everybody's a huckster on the Common. Kids who look like they just got off the bus from Akron wear "Get Smart, Get Prayer" T-shirts as they work the same street as the Hare Krishna crowd. A one-eyed fortune teller shares a stage with a pock-marked "folksinger" who intones that he was born too late, or too soon, or both.

And Bicentennial tourists, who have suddenly learned a new meaning for the term "Freedom Trail," stand and gawk, some of them undoubtedly hoping to God that nothing like this ever spreads to Boise. But if they feel too terribly out of place, a line of familiar faces waits directly across Tremont Street to welcome them home—McDonald's, Burger King, Papa Gino's, Baskin-Robbins and Dunkin' Donuts.

It's been this way on the Common ever since the town bought it from a local minister for thirty pounds in 1634. (Quite a buy, particularly when compared with the Frog Pond's new $228,000 ice-skating rink, which is uncovered, unfenced and barely covers one-fifth of an acre.) Society's undesirables traditionally have found a place here, though not always happily. Quakers and pirates were hanged on the field where cows once grazed. Deserters were shot, and various malcontents whipped. By the time the hippies arrived, during the famous summer of 1968, so had "civilization." So these intruders were merely chased away.

All this is not to say that you can't find rest and relaxation on the Common. There is, for instance, one particular pathway—stretching outward from Parkman Band Stand toward Central Burying Ground—which is the rallying point for several aging philosophers. They amble back and forth between benches, spreading the word.

The young zanies from up around Park street leave these elders alone, and the favor is returned. It is true that they might find even more serenity across Charles street in the Public Garden. But if it's not good enough for Tom the Oneman Band over there, it's not good enough for them, either.

COUNTRYSIDE / LIFESTYLES

I've Been a Fisherman All My Life

ENOUGH TIME—twenty years—has moved by since my life as a commercial fisherman to allow me to surprise new acquaintances with the information that indeed I did make my entire living as an independent harvester of the sea's bounty. "How did you ever get involved with something like that?" is the sort of question I hear these days whenever I mention my seven years spent pulling nets, pulling oars, pulling clam rakes, dredges and boats. I don't resent the surprise, or the questions. I know I don't look or act like a fisherman any more. I'm mostly a desk man now, complete with swivel chair and paunch.

But at this time of the year, that twenty years seems short. That's because I can still feel the tingle of adrenalin on these late

October mornings as I recall the vast migrations of striped bass that surged past our particular beach every autumn when October ended and November began. Each year, about now, millions of the fish flowed by like a river as what we called the "main body" of stripers took its annual journey south to the Chesapeake and the Hudson River.

If the elements allowed us—and the Atlantic was often its most awesome on those late fall days—we were offered the chance to gather our bumper crop, our "100-box haul" that we dreamt of so often. It came my way only once during my time on the water, but the excitement has hardly faded.

Assisted by photographs on my office walls I re-live those days many times in my mind's eye. And as I have over the years, I have come to realize that I have not moved as far from commercial fishing as my swivel chair and paunch might indicate.

It was an act of desperation which began my fishing career. Before I showed up on the beach that September two decades ago, I had been working as a public relations man in New York City. In my view, it was a disturbing occupation. I could see no true commodity being exchanged. Instead, I was paid to be clever, to be charming, to entertain, to flatter and to persuade. What writing I did had to be anonymous; what "work" I did could not possibly have been considered honest labor by most working people.

I became seriously depressed as these perceptions grew in validity. Finally, the circumstances seemed so pointless and so grim that I rushed from the city to the beach where I found the one person I knew there well enough to ask for help. He said he was going to try commercial fishing, and that I could join the crew.

From then on, I had no questions about the nature of my occupation. Together Jim and I rebuilt an ancient dory, together we restored a junked trailer to carry it, together we hung our nets from raw twine, ropes, corks and weights, and together we launched that dory in the open Atlantic on our first quest in the roaring surf.

66

When we caught fish (and that took a while) we heaved them into the truck, washed them, gutted them, weighed them and packed them in wooden boxes—125 pounds to a full box, complete with an additional 25 pounds of crushed ice.

Then we'd tag the boxes with the name and address of a wholesale dealer at the Fulton Fish Market in Manhattan, load the boxes back on the truck (and we never worked two men to a box) and take them over to Ted Lester's market in time to catch the big truck which would get our haul to the city. We had no way of knowing what we would be paid for our harvest; the price was set in the city by a system of supply and demand we neither understood nor could influence. In a week or so, our check would arrive in the mail, we'd split it even shares and keep on fishing. Every now and then, the price would be so low we'd get a bill for the freight instead of being paid; on the average, however, we would get a fair reward.

I liked that work. We were beholden to no one, our hours were our own, we made our own equipment, we depended on our own skills, we suffered from our own mistakes. We never saw the people who paid us for our goods; there was no such thing as politics or deals. Jim and I took our chances with the sea, the stripers and the storms. Our long, long days ended when we boxed, tagged and shipped our fish. Then it was time to start over.

As a writer, I have no crew, but that's about the only major difference. My fish don't swim in the sea; they are ideas and stories that swim everywhere. I must rely on my skills, my knowledge and my work to catch them. Once snared, I must put them in some order, package them and send them off in envelopes to editors I hardly know. If I've done my job, I get a check in the mail; if not, I get my fish back, worse for the wear. I am beholden to no one, work my own hours.

The people who learn of my sea-going past shouldn't be so surprised. After all, I'm still shipping fish.

Streets for Seeing
and Being Seen

PARIS. The typical American, whose basic view of urban living is that it's an appropriate way to learn guerrilla warfare, must make a certain adjustment when he or she arrives here. If you're used to treating city streets as the lairs of spiritless malcontents and raving crazies, the tendency is to run back to your hotel room at the first sign of sundown. In the United States, the Eleventh Commandment seems to be Thou Shalt Not Go Out After Dark, particularly if thou liveth in a place larger than Post Mills, Vt.

Parisians do not think that way about their city. Paris looks like what Boston would look like only if all the air conditioners broke down in August. I mean, the French people *go out*.

Now this is not *go out* in the sense of taking a family tour of the nearest Dairy Queen, or even going so far as to visit the local movie house. Nothing that formal, you understand. In Paris it's as if a whole segment of the population had suddenly and happily become homeless. At least that's the way it looks to an uninitiated visitor, because a conservative guess would be that a quarter of the people who live in Paris are walking, standing, or sitting in the streets at any given moment.

Part of this phenomenon is explained by the fact that many of the city's cafes are located on its sidewalks. They are what street corners used to be in America, before abandonment set in: places to relate stories, recall experiences or retell lies. People spend whole afternoons in cafes in Paris, lolling over a single glass of cognac and changing entire casts of fellow conversationalists. There is a rather rotund gentleman sitting in a cafe I know, Le Colibri, who appears not to have moved from his chair in three days. This is expected. Even the waiters tolerate it, which ought to tell me something about the differences between Paris and home.

But it is more than just the cafes. More than even the weather. In America (including Boston, with apologies to the North End), city streets are something to get away *from*, not *to*. They are looked upon the same way the townsfolk in western movies used to view Main street during a shoot-out. Grab the womenfolk and the children and get inside! In Paris, the streets are where you go to see and be seen, to bargain and to hassle, to laugh and to cry, to oh-h-h-h and to ah-h-h-h. When a Frenchman asks you to step outside, it isn't because he wants to beat you up. Compared to him and his kind, Boston is a city of shut-ins.

The best time to see all this, I can now reveal, is on July 14, better known as Bastille Day. After the tanks have paraded through the streets by day, everyone takes to them by night. Strolling along the Champs Elysees is a bit like making your way through Kenmore Square after a World Series game.

This year, around midnight, a group of thirty or so motorcyclists decided to pause in the midst of insane traffic and form a giant human pyramid so that one of their member might record the feat on film. A few drivers honked, a few passersby stopped to stare, but most people seemed not to notice. A pile of thirty human beings in the middle of the street in the middle of the night is simply nothing to get excited about in Paris.

COUNTRYSIDE / LIFESTYLES

The Long Days

How BRIEF are these nights, how langorous these days. The dawns and dusks seem to run together, shrinking the blackness until sleep becomes almost unnecessary in the luminous darks that tell us of summer's coming.

For me, there is particular joy in the late evenings and the early mornings. I can see the shining start of every dawning just a bit more than four hours after midnight, and the last rays of the setting sun do not vanish from a clear sky until nearly nine. That nearly sixteen hours of light is a restorative and a reassurance. It holds back the shadows of my anxieties that grow so long and threatening during the deep and endless darks of winter. In the sunlight, I see the loveliness of the world for what it is; during the long nights of December I see the creatures of my own imaginings and they are a comfortless crew.

There was a time decades ago when the confidence and ignorance of youth allowed me to sail innocently across such wide, black seas; but even when I was young I never failed to be exhilarated by May's lengthening days. Then I would live from dawn to dawn, running like a deer through time, never stopping for sleep and somehow finding sustenance in the excitement of the half-light that comes during these dusks and dawnings.

I may be no wiser now, but I am more regular. Whatever else the passing years may do, they cement routine, they impose their habits season after season until we become as regular as clocks, striking the hours with our times for rising, times for dining, times for washing, reading and worrying. We lose our limberness in this temporal tyranny. Whatever event or arrival or non-arrival disturbs the ritual of our routine breaks the order of the day as sharply and as painfully as a sudden fall might snap an old and brittle bone.

Until these days in May. Somehow the soaring sun lifts me out of the silly standards I have set the winter through. I am restored to the careless bravado I had as a boy; the shining hours of these long days illuminate some inner energy source that has gone untapped since last autumn. I am awake at five instead of seven; I go straight to the window to check the day's condition for fishing instead of lying abed pondering the condition of the roof. And, if the bay is spread there like a length of silver silk, I will leave the silent house for two or three stolen hours on the water before I get around to my more regular chores.

Just as often in the golden evenings I will return to the same waters I left ten hours before and I will drift in their caressing currents until the very last of the twilight leaves the western sky. Only then, using the lights in the house as my compass, will I steer for home and sup at an hour that would seem quite outlandish in December.

I am not alone in such soaring. The brilliance of this late spring light that sparks my restless exhuberance does the same for every natural creature in this land of long winters and short, sweet summers. There is no human or animal that I have seen which does not react just as a flower does, opening wide its blossoms, throwing back its arms, following the sun across its rising arc, reaching with intense vitality to break any bonds the now forgotten frosts may have left in place. We are all children of the light, and we draw our new strengths from the shared sense of excitement these long days bring.

You have only to listen to the birds to know of the vitality that so abounds. Like me, they start before the sun rises and, like me, they chatter long after it has set. There have been times when I have heard diurnal birds singing right along with the nocturnal owl, whippoorwill and night herons. I could understand. Like me, they are intoxicated with this season's luminescence. Just as I could not bring myself to stop running when I was a boy in May, these all-night birds can find no sense in observing routines set in another, grimmer season.

Their chatter excites me as soon as I open my eyes in the dawn. Their songs are part of the surging symphony of these days, and I can understand the sorrow of my aging neighbor whose growing deafness now prevents him from hearing the high frequencies of the song sparrow and the warbler. "How I wish I could hear those little birds," he says, meaning how he wishes he could still share that part of the excitement and adventure that are the gift of these bright hours.

Propping Up the Combat Zone

DEBRA BECKERMAN was immediately recognizable, principally because she was the one with clothes on. She was dressed in a black pantsuit and sitting in a small L-shaped dressing room at the rear of the "World Famous Two O'Clock Lounge," a strip joint located deep in Boston's Combat Zone. Of course, she does not like to hear it referred to as the Combat Zone, since she is annually paid $15,000 to get people to think of its bars, skin flicks, and porno book shops as making up the city's "adult entertainment district." Ms. Beckerman—a twenty-seven-year-old suburban mother from Waterville, Maine, who ran away to Las Vegas at age seventeen and later became a 96-cent-an-hour Playboy bunny—is the flack for legalized commercial sex in Boston. Employed by the Lower Washington Street Business Association, she is sort of the Ron Ziegler of the Hub. This we had to see.

"They're not doing it because they want to be naked in front of men," she explained earnestly when we joined her as she sat on a trunk located among several female forms in various states of undress. "They're doing it to make a living." We nodded seriously. One of the *theys*, Corinne Alphen, twenty-two, was standing behind Ms. Beckerman. She was there literally in the flesh, the very same flesh which had recently caused her to be crowned none other than Miss Nude International in Atlantic City. "I feel I'm entertaining when I'm out there," she proclaimed softly. "I have an audience. A stage. A wardrobe. A spotlight. You know, a little glitter and a little glamour make you feel like a real showgirl." Again we nodded knowingly, this time trying to avert our eyes.

Ms. Beckerman, meanwhile, continued our education, which apparently had been neglected. "My biggest problem," she complained, "is getting respect for the people who do business here. What are they doing that's any less respectable than what Jordan

Marsh is doing?" Search us, we replied. After all, it's been three years since the Supreme Court ruled that obscenity should be defined by "community" standards. A year after that, the Boston Zoning Commission designated the Combat Zone a first-in-the-nation adult entertainment district. Why, even the Boston Redevelopment Authority is in on the act now, having come up with a sign code for the Zone. With Ms. Beckerman trundling off with strippers—sorry, "dancers"—to talk to everyone from Sonja Hamlin to the Kiwanis Club, can apple pie be far behind?

"Do you know who the average guy is who comes to the Two O'Clock?" she asked. By now we expected he was a scout master and, wouldn't you know, we weren't far off. "He's thirty-five to fifty years old, happily married, and an electrical engineer," she announced. Putting aside the question of precisely how one averages out to be an electrical engineer, we inquired as to whether Ms. Beckerman thought she was peddling a rather sad form of fantasy. We wondered particularly about the "mixers" who are employed in clubs such as the Two O'Clock to entice customers into buying them $6 drinks.

"It's entirely fantasy," she replied. "But what's so bad about it? Look, there are lots of lonely men in the world who are not particularly super at communicating. They're the kind who, if they go to a dating bar, are going to get rejected. In a place like this, they don't even have to move; the ladies come and talk to them. And they don't have to worry about being rejected. Some men just like to be able to say they bought a drink for Miss Nude International."

Speaking of the devil, Miss N.I. herself was about to go on stage. As she oozed into her costume, we explained that we would have to skip the show, and she seemed genuinely disappointed. But we promised to return another time.

Outside, Debra Beckerman stood on Washington street, looking past the marquee for "Slippery When Wet" and up toward the proudly proclaimed Dirty Book Store. Beyond that stood the All Nude Tobacco Shop. "The people who own these businesses make a lot of money," she admitted. "It's a very, very lucrative business. This is becoming a camp place to go. Some nights it actually gets overrun with couples." For the first time, she seemed concerned. "Of course," she exclaimed, "we wouldn't want to go too far. I mean, we've got to keep it questionable, don't we?"

COUNTRYSIDE / LIFESTYLES

Tides and Days

THIS YEAR—and every other—would be bleaker indeed if I did not have my tide calendar. Perhaps tide calendar is not the proper technical designation; perhaps I should say tide table. But I'm not sure that would be correct, either. I have seen some tide tables (like those in the U.S. Coast and Geodetic Society reference books) which would give me headaches whenever I tried to compute the best spring afternoon for launching the boat.

The tide calendars I'm talking of are published by considerate folks who have already done the work of deciphering the Geodetic Survey logarithms; instead of headaches I get a tidy set of data and a clear and readable chart which tells me the time of low and high tides, the phase of the moon, and the height of the tide—plus and minus. The date and day of the week are thrown in for good measure with the result that just about everything a fellow needs to know (including times for sunrise and sunset, which I forgot to mention) is there on one small page.

I keep the tide calendar just by the stove in our kitchen. In the morning, just as the coffee goes on, I get a scan of the next twenty-four hours. It's always a help. I have argued for years, for example, that storm systems, especially New England's coastal storms, move in coordination with the tides. In my amateur meteorological logic, storms peak with the high tide and recede with the low—well, more often than not, anyway. So even though the bay is locked in ice and the tides race invisibly beneath this mantle, I feel better knowing when high tide will come. Then, if Don Kent tells me a nor'easter is on the way, I expect its worst moments to coincide with the times on my tide calendar. I am prepared psychologically, at least.

On bright days, low tide is important. Then I know when it is safe to go skating on the bay—a feat I would never attempt if salt water rolled under the ice. But no one was ever hurt, were they, by falling through the ice to a mud flat. At low tide, there are miles of mud flats where I can skate safely and with abandon.

But even beyond the interest I apply to tidal research is the eagerness with which I follow the phases of the moon—especially in these months of deep winter. This week, alas, we are essentially without a moon. There is a large, round, black, moon-faced dot on the tide calendar which tells me so. It means that December's moon (full Christmas night) has waned away, and January's new moon has yet to show.

That new moon will be along before we know it. I will watch for it, slim, curved and silver cold there in the western sky just at sunset. My grandfather told me that if you looked at a new moon first over your left shoulder and jingled the silver coins in your pocket at the same time, you would grow richer before the moon was full. So I watch for the new moon, walking backwards towards our point, looking over my left shoulder and jingling a few dimes. It's amazing on how many evenings clouds have obscured my view. Discouraged, I let go my dimes and turn around so I can walk properly. Then the new moon slides out from behind the clouds, telling me once again that I should have been more persistent, more determined—and that's a good lesson, regardless; liable, even, to make a fellow some money.

In the winter, the full moon is at its best, so I watch the tide calendar for the nights when the large, white, moon-faced dot shows up. You can have your summer moons with their mush, their romance and their soft light. I'll take the winter moons every time, with their hard edges, their brilliant silver light, and reflections on a thousand, glazed snowdrifts in the field. Winter moons make blue shadows on the snow; there is no such summer miracle.

In these Maine skies, winter moons also illuminate the weather. I have stood just outside our door and looked up to the full-moon sky to see one set of clouds moving in from the west at the same time a second set races from the east. Both of them meet and cross below my hard, winter moon, and from my own back door, I watch the heavens spin. Bereft of my tide calendar, I might not even have known the moon would be full.

The First and Last All-Night Restaurant Awards

ONE OF the late George Frazier's many laments was that he could not get anything to eat in Boston at five o'clock in the morning. Frazier, of course, was dealing on his own terms. You can get *food*. It's just that you might not want to *eat* it.

I know this not because I am nocturnal or insomnious. I know it because I recently spent a midnight-to-dawn shift in no fewer than eleven urban twenty-four-hour eateries, a record of which any cab driver would be proud. (It actually was an even dozen stops, if you choose to count the vending machines at the all-night Boston Bowl in Dorchester.)

I stared into the jaws of reused grease, listened to the vague ramblings of assorted strangers and was serenaded by everyone from a drunk on an adjoining stool to Vickie Sue Robinson on the jukebox. I am here to tell you and George Frazier that this long night's journey into day proved nothing else if not the fact that time in 'round-the-clock restaurants is measured not by the moon and the stars. Instead, it is counted by the sound of trucks bringing the morning editions of the city's dailies.

While you ponder that particular homily, consider the following as the First and Last Annual Boston All-Night Restaurant Awards:

Best Dancers. Howard Johnson's, 500 Boylston St. Dancers? It had never occurred to me that you could do the hustle to Muzak until visiting this well-disguised disco at 4 A.M. Boylston's desperados have become firmly entrenched among the twenty-eight flavors.

Most Cabbies. Hayes Bickford's, 133 Causeway St. Like grown-up teenagers, they lounge on hoods and against fenders, occasionally stepping inside for coffee and English. The counterman knows the regulars, whose orders are cooking even as they walk through the door.

Worst Menu Item. Buzzy's Roast Beef, 327 Cambridge St. You have never really died until served a fifty-cent stuffing sandwich shoved through a small window by a hairy arm. It's enough to make the next door neighbors in the Charles St. Jail glad they're eating in.

Best Entertainment (Planned). Mike's Deli, 199 Essex St. The jukebox isn't bad (they're not easy to find at dawn), and the Captain Fantastic pinball machine will help get you through the night (lean heavily on the left side). If these don't keep you awake, the thirty-cent whole dill pickles surely will.

Best Entertainment (Unplanned). Hi-Deli Sandwich Board, 180 Federal St. Characters, characters. Rootless toters of shopping bags and assorted zanies. One aging gentleman regaled me with the story of Richard Nixon's plot to buy the Catholic Church. Even the help is spacy.

Most Waiters Per Square Foot. Kim Toy Restaurant, corner of Tyler and Beach Sts. They come at you from so many angles you think you're in an automobile showroom. One brings the menu, another the water, another the silverware, etc. All Chinatown seems to pass the night here, either eating or on the payroll.

Most Interesting. The Englewood Diner, 1895 Dorchester Ave. This is the real thing: an authentic old wooden diner, a one-person staff and seating for thirty-two. With its bright outside lights flooding deserted Peabody Square, the Englewood is a lot like eating on the outskirts of New Bedford.

Least Interesting. Four-way tie among the Howard Johnson's Restaurants on the Southeast Expressway and at 944 Morrissey Blvd. in Dorchester and the Dunkin' Donuts shops at 951 Bennington St. in East Boston and 875 Morrissey Blvd. in Dorchester. The only thing I found interesting at any of these was the counterfeit $5 bill used by a Dunkin' Donuts customer in Eastie. He got away with it.

COUNTRYSIDE / LIFESTYLES

Lured by Islands

FOR YEARS I have believed what I heard or read so long ago that I have since forgotten: there are 365 islands in Maine's Casco Bay—thus the term "Calendar Islands." When I finally get that summer vacation (and I've been in Maine twenty years without one) I may spend it counting islands in this bay that reaches to the edge of our home. And if I get another vacation after that, I may try visiting and counting every one of the islands along the Maine coast. There are, I've been told, more than a thousand.

I can't vouch for that. I can only talk with some reliability of the islands I can see from our windows on a clear day—probably ten or eleven, if you count the smallest. I can throw a stone across that one. I've sailed among these islands, rowed past them, walked to

78

them over the salt ice in the deepest winters. I watch them begin to glow with the season when they become green in the spring, and then grow golden in the fall as the birch and aspen turn.

In the summer, on these days in late July when the season has matured to its richest, the largest of the islands are thick with the extravagance of their forests. The growth is so lush, the shrubs so expansive that walking in island woods becomes difficult—a trip into darkness, even on the brightest days.

I suppose this is one of the reasons why Maine's islands have always been the favorites of summer visitors, especially those who arrive by boat. Not a July weekend goes by when the masts of several sloops, schooners, yawls, and ketches aren't waving along the patch of horizon I can see from our yard. Often I'll turn around an island point, rowing the dory in the early morning, and find the cove I left empty the day before has filled with cruisers—power boats that arrive in groups, like bikers on their cycles, or vanners in their vans.

Most of the yachtsmen and the cruising skippers go ashore, with their families, friends, children, and—every now and then—the seagoing family pet. And I'm sure that when they do, almost every one of them believes himself or herself to be on a deserted island. That's the wonder of these places; they have this awesome ability to recuperate, to somehow retain their purity even though hundreds of skiffs have been hauled up on the rocky beaches and thousands of hamburgers and hotdogs have been charred over driftwood fires.

There is something in every human, young and old, that thrills in setting foot on a bit of land that is wild, free and alone. There is a universal excitement and delight in finding a spot that is unexplored and uninhabited. That is the lure of these Maine islands, and the wonder is that they can still appear so wild and free after being visited so regularly by so many tens of thousands of folks from Salisbury and Saugus.

It is the sea that is the purifier. In October and November, wind-borne tides wash the island shores clean, and in December and January, snow scours the land. From one summer to the next, the islands emerge as clean as desert bones, ready for yet another invasion of adventurers whose fantasies are fulfilled by the thought that theirs are the only footprints in the sand.

Which is not so, of course. There is a house on the west shore of one of the islands I can see. On the eastern side, red cliffs rise steeply, pushed suddenly from the sea in a past glacial spasm. A thin strand of pebbled beach borders the cliff base; at middle tide it is just wide enough for a driftwood fire. Because the red cliffs rise straight from a deep water channel well marked on the charts, the thin beach is a favorite of cruising parties.

I watch as they probe the channel cautiously, then drop anchor just off the island. The dinghies are lowered and yet another landing is made, the fire is built and the hamburgers charred. Then, as the rising tide begins to roll and the beach begins to shrink, the dinghies return to their mother ships, the anchors are weighed and the summer fleet sets sail.

I'm certain that each of the sailors is sure that he has set foot on a wild place. Yet, if they had climbed the cliffs, or taken their boats across the shoals, they would have seen the home of a fellow man. The great thing about these Maine islands is, however, that none of the fellows was, or will be, aware of the other's presence. Which is why I'd like to visit them all.

CITYSIDE / LIFESTYLES

A Day at the Comic Book Collector's Market

THE KID took the steps at Boston's Arlington Station three at a time, hitting the street in full stride. He pushed his hands into the pockets of his fake leather jacket, strode quickly across the near-empty square, and entered the Statler Hilton without glancing at the doorman. Inside, he immediately bounded down the stairs to the Bay State Room and fished a dollar from his jeans. "I'm looking for Powerman," the kid said to the young woman who took his money. "You seen any Powerman?"

On principle, we usually try to stay away from comic book freaks. For one thing, their view of history tends to be a bit distorted. To such "panelologists," the month of June 1945 is notable not for the signing of the United Nations Charter, but as the month Little Lulu made her debut in comic-book form. Comic collectors are also willing to debate such momentous issues as whether Spiderman dealt with the Scorpion in January—or February—of 1965.

Nevertheless, we recently decided to accept the kid's invitation to join him on his regular trek to the Comic Book Collector's Market, which is held roughly once a month at the Statler. It is the result of the "Second Heroic Age of Comics," a phenomenon which is attracting folks not only to two such regular commercial happenings in the Hub, but also to similar goings-on in such outlying cities as Providence and Hartford.

"But before we go there's one thing we gotta get straight," the kid had insisted prior to leaving his home in the suburbs. 'The Coming of the Scorpion' appeared in Spiderman in *January* 1965, OK?" We assured him it was all right with us.

Once inside the hotel, the kid went to work. About 200 people milled around twenty or so tables seeking treasure. Fingers flipped through cardboard boxes neatly filled with protective plastic sleeves. They flicked a Sgt. Fury here, stopped at a Mighty Thor there. On one wall, a Batman No. 9 was going for $90. On another, Wonder Woman No. 7 was fetching $50.

"I'm strictly into PM," the kid said, worming his way towards a table. PM? "Pristine mint condition," he answered. "I usually don't get into the high dollar stuff. But a couple of weeks ago I paid $60 for Reform School Girl, a one-shot from 1951. The cover says it's 'The graphic story of boys and girls running wild in the violence-ridden slums of today.' Far out."

81

We left the kid to his wanderings and looked up Stan Darcy, the 48-year-old entrepreneur behind the Collector's Market. Occasionally fingering his pencil-thin mustache, Darcy explained that he owns a paperback and joke shop in Brockton and has been attracting people like the kid to the Statler for four years.

"It's mostly a teen market," he conceded, "but for older collectors the prices are fantastic. An Action No. 1—that was the first appearance of Superman, back in 1938 I think it was—is worth $5000. In five or ten years it may be worth $25,000."

But maybe not, if we take the word of Stan Hager, a dealer from Beverly. "The dealers have priced themselves into a corner," he told us as we tried to locate the kid. "The 'Golden Age' stuff from the 1940s has leveled off in the past year. The '60s stuff is still going up, though not as fast as it was. The combination of dealer greed and collector stupidity has been very discouraging. It's priced the younger people out of the business."

Not all of them, we hasten to add. For out there on the faded red carpet was the persevering kid. "The guy's right," he said when we told him what Hager had said. "This is getting to be big money now. Fat city. But you can still get a lot of stuff for a buck or two. I got my Powerman today for a good price. And a PM Spiderman. And lookit this: eight Little Lulus for my kid sister. Four bucks total. When she's my age they'll probably be worth ten times that much." Smiling, the kid pushed the comic books under his arm, said good-bye, and went off to take the Green Line out of town.

COUNTRYSIDE / LIFESTYLES

The Summer Set

OUR SUMMER neighbors are packing to leave, and I shall miss them. Unlike some summer visitors, these have been a daily source of entertainment, education, and delight—and they have never once asked to borrow our lawnmower or awakened us at night with sounds of uninhibited revelry.

These neighbors are waterborne; they are the eider ducks who nest on the solitary shores of the small island just visible from our windows. At dead low tide, anyone who wants to sink to his knees in primordial ooze can easily walk from our place to the island, but for the eiders it must seem a safe nursery. They have returned every year now for the past three summers to raise their considerable families.

The result has been the same sort of geometric progression that affects other summer resorts of desirability. The eiders "discovered" Crow Island with the same sort of enthusiasm the first arrivals from New York must have "discovered" Bar Harbor. Two eider hens stumbled on the place in the summer of '75; they raised their considerable broods (about twelve to sixteen ducklings each) and departed.

They must have been gabby birds. Their tales of "where we spent last summer . . ." probably echoed through the ranks of the huge flocks that winter in the open ocean off Scituate and Cohasset, because when the '76 season began in June, there were six or seven hens paddling around Crow looking for summer rentals. Those same determined mothers hatched at least a total of eighty eider offspring, and by the summer of '77, the entire Middle Bay region was laboring under an eider invasion.

Obviously every choice spot on Crow had been leased before the original eiders had left the preceding September, so the latecomers had to shift for themselves when it came to finding accommodations in other parts of the bay. There are now eider summer colonies established on Scragg Island, Barnes Point, and, for all I know, way up in Skolfield's Cove. Like the folks in Bar Harbor, Seal Harbor, Manset, and Northeast Harbor, the various Middle Bay eider communities keep pretty much to themselves, gathering just once or twice a season for a mussel contra dance, or some such event.

So popular a spot has Middle Bay become for these large and

deliberate sea ducks that during the season just past, I could see an eider flock anytime I looked out the window. I watched the first hens arrive in June (a bit late this year, but then wasn't everyone) and it wasn't long before they paraded their broods the entire length of the cove, almost as if they were passing in review, proud of their maternal accomplishment.

The ducklings then were about the size of tennis balls, and their natural buoyancy was almost more than they could handle. Trying to dive with all the determination their mothers insisted on, the child eiders would disappear for a moment or two beneath the bay's still waters and then break the surface, popping like released balloons from below, looking for all the world as if they were about to bounce into the air. Some of the youngsters must have felt a bit sheepish, watching parent birds submerge for minutes on end, resurfacing with the ease and aplomb of a porpoise.

Through June, July, August and September, I watched the broods grow until it has become impossible to tell mother from child—at least from a distance. Every now and then, when I take the dory for a row, my course intersects with that of an eider flotilla. As they give way, I can see that some of the birds are responding to signals from one or two others; I can hear the guttural calling. The young birds do as they're told, either dispersing and diving, or bunching and paddling. The latter tactic creates a moving cluster of feathers that I have clocked at better than five knots, and the wake has nudged yachts at anchor.

Ours has never been a lonely spot; the natural world never is. But with the eiders as company during the summer, a good many smiles have been added to our days. I wonder, however, about the future. According to my projections, the eider population has now reached critical mass. If all the birds that are about to leave us take the message of Middle Bay back to the wintering grounds, the situation here next June will be definitely chaotic. We will be witness to nothing less than a summer housing crisis. We'll have to wait and see how the birds work it out; meanwhile, it will be a longer winter without them.

84

The Duke of Panhandling Eyes the Bottom Line

IF YOU think Christmas is a crucial time of year solely for Jordan Marsh and Filene's, you should talk to Duke. He does business right up the street from the two downtown department stores at the intersection of a pair of footpaths on Boston Common. If shopping is off in December, Duke and his wife and kids may not see the Bahamas in January. Being a professional panhandler is enough to make you sweat bullets.

"An excellent year so far," Duke admitted the other morning from beneath his tattered wool cap. "It looks like my net earnings and profits per share will reach a new high, despite the problems of diversification. I've got my kid working the corner of Tremont and Boylston streets, you know."

The operation sounded impressive. But we wondered precisely how this year compared to other years. Duke scratched the gray stubble on his face, searching for the right words.

"As you know," he finally replied, "the last three years were marked by spiraling costs and recession. Businesses everywhere . . ."

Here Duke had to pause a moment to shuffle with outstretched hand toward a well-dressed businessman. The gentleman quickened his pace and brushed past Duke, almost knocking him over.

". . . were affected and panhandling was no exception," he said as he walked back toward us. "But last year the challenges were met and the picture began to turn around. I think accelerating my marketing program had a lot to do with it."

Your marketing program?

"Well certainly," he replied, pulling a soiled handkerchief from his pocket and wiping his runny nose. "I felt I needed better balance to appeal to different kinds of customers. Of course, my

85

point of most intense concentration is still the middle income businessman, despite periodic downtrends in that particular market segment."

Duke again lurched across the path and loomed up in front of a young couple. Almost in self-defense, the man handed him a coin.

"Damn," said Duke softly as the couple scurried away. "A Canadian quarter. The adverse impact of fluctuations in foreign currencies is definitely a negative factor. Luckily, my material costs are minimal, so my gross margins don't erode. But God knows it's not easy."

What about Christmas, we asked.

Duke shifted from one cloth-wrapped foot to the other. "It's definitely the key," he answered. "Right now I look solid in all the majors: earnings before taxes, taxes on earnings, net earnings and net earnings per share. I mean, all my gains are in line with the objectives I set for myself this year, you know?"

Duke rolled his red eyes toward the heavens. "But the next three weeks—twenty-one days, my friend—will determine what kind of an annual meeting we have. Snow can kill you in this business. Rain is your constant enemy. In other words, weather is a totally unpredictable variable which can't be programmed into your analytical projections."

Before departing, we told Duke we wanted him to give us a preview of next year, inasmuch as many of the so-called "experts" are uncertain about the immediate future.

"I think we can look ahead to next year with confidence," he said, eyeing an approaching middle-aged man who was wearing an expensive coat with a fur collar. "As for me, my objective is naturally to increase my net earnings while keeping operating costs in check. And then, who knows? Maybe in a couple more years my kid can move up here to this spot. The trend is toward multinationals, my friend, and that's a young man's game. Me, I'd rather be in the Bahamas."

And with that, Duke veered toward the approaching figure, muttering maniacally about twenty-five cents for a cup of coffee. The poor guy never had a chance.

An Owl in Midwinter

THESE ARE short days, and dusk comes so early it often slips by me and night appears suddenly on the doorstep, requiring lights lit, fires built and supper served. On the one or two days a week when I am at home, I resent night's rude intrusion, untempered by the stillness of dusk. I watch, if I am splitting wood by the barn—which is my regular, winter chore and productive substitute for jogging—for the setting sun. Unless I am too stubbornly in contest with a knotted log that will not split as planned, or diverted by the unannounced visit of a neighbor, I leave what I am doing when the western sky grows red and walk to the rim of the bay to sit quietly as the brief dusk deepens overhead. It is a peaceful time, without horizons, when all images are softened.

Dusk slipped by me a week or so ago, yet I went to the point, unwilling to let night take every quiet moment. Only a brush stroke of twilight was left at the rim of the western woods; the trees on the point were dark patterns against a dark sky. As I got closer to them, one dead branch rattled against another overhead—a sound like two dry bones clattering. I looked up as a large owl took wing, no more than ten feet above me. Like the trees themselves, he was a dark, but fluid shape against a darkening sky.

His wings moved without a sound; he flew through the air over me as silently as a fish swims beneath the surface of a clear sea. To me, the soundless flight was incredible; even sparrows buffet the air as they take wing; the whistle of wind through a duck's pinions can be heard for some distance, yet here was this huge bird—its wings spread as wide as my outstretched arms—and I heard not a whisper of feathers on the air. Had it not been for the dry oak branch which sprang upwards against its neighbor when the owl left its perch, I never would have looked up, never would have known the creature was within my ken. Like the dusk itself, he would have slipped away unnoticed.

It was a great horned owl, and although I tried to follow his flight, he vanished quickly in a pine grove; but, coincidentally, not from my consciousness. Oh, I would have remembered the moment; I don't come upon that many wild creatures in such proximity not to have remembered. But there was more to our meeting than that.

Within a day or so, a farming friend asked me what it was that could be killing her bantam hens. They roost, she said, in the top of a tall, ancient lilac planted a century ago in the farmstead dooryard. Twenty feet up, they roost, and each night for the past five nights, one has been taken. On the sixth evening, just at dusk, the farmer saw a large bird glide from the woods across the road; another bantam was taken.

"You wouldn't believe the size of that bird," the farmer said, holding her arms outstretched.

"Yes, I would," I said, explaining that I had just recently seen the same kind of bird (but quite likely not the same individual) about ten feet over my head.

The next morning I stopped at the library to learn more. "Birds Of America" told me that both my farming friend and I had been visited by no less than the "tiger of the air . . . The sweep of his great wings in the silent air is as noiseless as the tread of the big cat's padded feet on the soft earth . . . and the murderous clutch of his great talons are as pitiless as the spring of the tiger upon the helpless lamb . . . To the poultry farmer, the great horned owl is a terror; once he has acquired a preference for domestic fowls, nothing short of death is likely to deter him . . ."

So much for the bantams. I learned a good deal more about my awesome visitor, and I have been hoping to see him yet again. I haven't, not so far, and soon, according to my newly acquired knowledge, my chances will grow increasingly slim. The great horned owl, says "Birds Of America," lays its eggs as early as the last week in January. "It is by no means uncommon (I now know) to find a great horned owl stolidly incubating under a thick blanket of snow."

Now there is a thought for all of us who find no hope of spring in January. The great horned owl knows better, and for me that is a wonderful reason for walking to the point at dusk, even when it has all but slipped by me on these short, cold days.

CITYSIDE / LIFESTYLES

Dog Days

ON BEACON Hill, they are obsessed by it. In Back Bay, they are possessed by it. Throughout The Fenway, they are placed in stress by it. What it is, of course, is obvious. In Rome it was called *excrementum canis*. Our own expression for it is somewhat less formal, but we may assume that Bostonians hold stepping in it to be as equally distasteful as did the Romans.

Of course, certain Boston neighborhoods have other things to worry about—crime, taxes, potholes and the like. Yet, through the years, the subject keeps cropping up in newspapers, elections and community meetings. In 1975, it was actually the subject of both a campaign press release from Mayor Kevin White and a deadly serious editorial in the Boston *Globe*. But perhaps the staunchest anti-mess advocate was the suburban dog officer who stood up at a State House hearing ten years ago and advocated the writing of tickets for misbehaving canines.

The idea was clearly ahead of its time. Were such a proposal put forth today, it would undoubtedly have no trouble finding a responsive legislature. How foolish we've been all these years, having meter maids run around ticketing automobiles. Had they spent their time more purposefully, chasing Chihuahuas and Dobermans instead of Chevies and Dodges, the city would clearly be a better place in which to live.

89

If we'd only acted when that first warning flare was sent aloft we could have developed an entire bureaucracy of dog chasers by now. And what with no-bid contracts and nepotism, it seems quite possible that the elite Dog Officers Guard (DOG), armed to the teeth with that ultramodern weapon known as the pooper scooper, might today rival the Boston Police Department's famed and feared Tactical Patrol Force.

But our priorities got—if you'll pardon the expression—all fouled up. We considered whether or not to build Park Plaza or a new Charles Street Jail when we should have been contemplating the questions of *excrementum canis*. Great minds debated busing when they could have been arguing the merits of chemical toilets for pooches. (Such a product was actually introduced a few years back, but Boston was obviously too busy entertaining such crackpot schemes as the Denver Boot to consider it.) Before we knew it there was an authentic crisis: a "crap gap," which is not unlike a missile gap, only much worse. To put it in the words of one articulate Boston official: "You ask me, the whole thing stinks."

Frankly, we couldn't have said it better ourselves. In London, where the police don't even carry guns, it's illegal for dogs to befoul footpaths. Can you imagine the additional law enforcement impact of a .45? Consider the pekingese which, prepared to relieve itself on a public way, is suddenly confronted by the wrong end of a gun barrel. Maybe a little law and order is just what this town needs.

The bleeding hearts, of course, will try to claim the *owners* are the ones who are at fault. But don't you believe them. A German shepherd is just as capable of distinguishing right from wrong as you or me. The whole thing has absolutely nothing to do with obedience training.

For a while recently, Boston had an Animal Control Commission not unlike the one proposed on a statewide basis a decade ago. But if you telephone City Hall now in search of that particular agency you will be told to call the Police Department with your particular "animal complaints." Maybe that's a sign that the city, finally realizes *excrementum canis* is a serious law and order issue best left in the hands of hardened professionals. Those people in Back Bay, The Fenway and Beacon Hill know what they're talking about. Let's get down to business and stop, ah, sidestepping the issue.

COUNTRYSIDE / LIFESTYLES

Families of All Kinds

I'M PLEASED to see the family—lately sociologists and assorted academics have been calling it the "nuclear" family—holding up under the recent pressures to make it an obsolete institution. There was a time there a few years back when every other publication carried an article on the demise of the nuclear family. It is a demise which never occurred and which I never believed was about to. On one hand, I couldn't surmise what could take the family's place. Mothers, fathers, brothers, sisters, grandparents, aunts and uncles and other relatives do, after all, constitute a kind of irreducible community which functions as an operating social unit geared to the survival of each member. If the unit design is shattered, then so too are the crucial patterns for survival.

And besides, the dissolution of the family wouldn't be natural. I can argue that case with more conviction at this time of the year than any other, having just watched a number of natural families evolve over the summer. There is, for one, the osprey couple and their only fledgling—a rather awkward child whose parents spent most of the summer teaching to fish. Ospreys are not social birds; their nest is perched in a tall pine on an island about a mile from our place. Unless you know just where to look, you could sail right by the pine and never spot the nest. But, every now and then, when the tide is right and the alewives or mackerel are about, the ospreys come to our cove for dinner.

Usually they sweep over, hang there, hovering on their broad wings until their telescopic eyes find a fish loafing in the shallows. The wings fold back, the bird becomes projectile, dropping like a feathered bomb that explodes in a white splash. More often than not, the osprey will emerge, struggling just a bit, with a fish in its talons. With a mighty beating of wings, it rises, free of the water, shakes dry, and then takes slow, labored strokes toward the island, the airborne fish catching the sun like a silver plate.

But with their child, the parents are more repetitive. They dive, but pull out at the last second; they are, I have surmised, showing the youngsters how. Then the fledgling tries; it is a dive without grace, but an impressive, thumping splash when the bird hits the water. I'm sure, if I'd had the time, I could have witnessed the proud moment when the fledgling first caught its own dinner.

I have seen young crows being fed by both parents, early in the morning when the birds assume we humans are not about. The adolescent crows are whiners, that's for sure, but their mewling caws have gotten more substantial with each passing week; now that Labor Day is here I can hardly tell the young from the adult, even though the birds that hatched last spring still follow their parents, hoping for a handout. The feedings which I witnessed in early July, however, have stopped. The older crows know that after autumn comes the winter, and woe unto any crow who hasn't learned to fend for itself by then.

There have been many such families. In the bay, mother eiders swim with massive broods of up to fifteen ducklings. The parent birds spent most of June battling great black-back gulls, keeping them from downing a baby eider in one cruel gulp. Now the youngsters are flipping their wings, getting ready to head for the eider wintering grounds of Massachusetts. It's the same with the teal and black duck on the woods pond, the deer and her twin fawns, the moose couple and their lurching calf.

Less than a year from now, the young that we watched this

summer will be adults; they will be beginning families of their own. The process is a cycle as eternal as the phases of the moon or the turning of the earth, and from it has come the survival of the species. When the sons and daughters leave in the autumn, it does not mean the family unit has been dissolved; it means only that the way for more families has been cleared. We, humankind, are natural beings as much as the deer and the osprey. Those who so confidently predicted the family's demise should have spent more time watching the ospreys.

CITYSIDE / LIFESTYLES

London Gripes Make Yanks Feel at Home

LONDON. So much for the notion of "swinging sophisticated London." King's road has about as much to do with the true fabric of London as Newbury street has to do with an accurate sense of Boston. Many Londoners are frightened by their own metropolis, and not just because the lack of rain is causing lager beer shortages while threatening to turn Regent's Park into a facsimile of Crane's Beach.

London seems to be using the same public-relations firm as most of the cities in the United States. Except for crime (they *do* worry about it, but at least they can still call it "vandalism"), it seems to hold all the real and imagined terrors of its counterparts in the colonies. We Americans can find comfort in the knowledge that we have not quite cornered the market on fear of urban living.

Like Boston, London is viewed in the hinterlands as a place populated by people who haven't the means or the good sense to pack up and get out. Even worse, it is looked upon by many of its inhabitants as a Rube Goldberg device to which the operating instructions have somehow been misplaced. They feel they are losing their grip on their destinies just as the Crown lost its grip on the world.

The parallels to America are enough to make you think there never was a War for Independence. You inevitably discover them at teatime, which is when the pace in England moves from slower to slowest. Everyone takes time out to get civilized, and the tradition becomes the perfect vehicle for bemoaning the changes which are felt to be altering London as radically as did the blitz.

They don't use polite American news media terms like "changing neighborhoods," but that's what they mean. The corner grocer has been moved out by the new housing project. The local school is suspected of being run by a bunch of freaks who don't know the meaning of the word discipline. The people next door have found a house in the suburbs, and the rumor is that the new family is not of British stock. For a country raised to believe that salvation is achieved by preserving the status quo, these changes are viewed as sure signs of the pathway to hell.

As is the case in America, the inflation rate in England is not likely to improve one's disposition. The downtrodden economy just makes everything appear that much worse. But it's not easy, while contemplating a pint of bitter in a London pub, to blame your troubles on something as the real GNP or the lack of stimulative fiscal proposals. Scapegoats are more useful when they're closer at hand.

In London's case, that means immigration. "Heathrow Airport looks like New Delhi" is one local's lament. Another tells me that "between the bloody tourists and the bloody Indians, there are none of us left." The newspapers are full of wailing and counterwailing about the alleged laxness of the country's immigration laws. One Londoner has become something of a folk hero by offering his house for sale to an "English family only."

The fear of "outsiders" coming in and routing whole neighborhoods by their mere presence is something a Bostonian can identify with. I happen to be staying in the Islington section of London, a polyglot which no one will ever confuse with Mayfair. I like it just fine, but the charming woman next door—who has lived in the same house since 1918—has spent more than one teatime serving me tales of the way it *used* to be. Meaning, of course, British.

So another city takes its knocks. Its middle- and lower-class residents are angry and frustrated, wishing they could take the Underground to paradise and abandon London to whomever wins the subsequent war between the "bloody tourists" and the "bloody Indians." It's enough to make an American feel right at home.

Coping

COUNTRYSIDE / COPING

Chores and Kids

A FELLOW ISN'T likely to realize just how many chores a country place imposes until he tries to do them all single-handed. Well, I'd better restate that, and fast. A couple isn't likely to comprehend the incredible number of things around the place that need doing until that couple—the lazy man and the hard-working wife—have to get them done without much help.

I suppose I've been more spoiled than most. There was a time there, and it seems like yesterday, when I could look around the breakfast table at the healthy bodies and not-so-smiling faces of at least five young men and women. And they were mine, captive labor, unable to extricate themselves—no matter what the excuse—from at least a couple of hours of work around the place. Oh, were those ever the days! Before I left the house for a grueling assignment like covering a fashion show or interviewing a summer theater star, I could tick off all that I wanted accomplished in my absence.

99

"Mow the lawn. Clip the long grass around the terrace wall. Repair the broken step. Haul out the dory and scrape her bottom clean. Weed the vegetable garden. Split more wood for the winter. Wash the car ...." and so it went. Very often our own five, muscular teen-agers, would augment their force with several free-loading friends, come to swimming or play volleyball. They would be pressed into service along with the others. It was amazing how much could be done within a relatively short time span.

The trouble is, I never realized just how much was being done. As far as I was concerned in those days, the young were lazy, incredibly so, and worked as if they were rehearsing for lead parts in a slow-motion film. I was, of course, quite wrong. There was a high quotient of raw energy compressed within those sinewy frames, and, given the proper incentive (as in wanting to get the chore done in time to catch the high tide at the beach) it could move mountains. I would return in the evening mulling an interview and, lo and behold, at least half of my morning assignments would be completed. As a crew foreman for slave labor, I was batting .500, and that's not bad.

Often, however, instead of being grateful for the work that had been done, I would rant about what hadn't. I suppose this ritual was something of a strain for all concerned, but it did wonders for the proper maintenance of the place and its accessories. Now that most of my slaves have flown, I often have only myself to rant at, and you would be surprised at how quickly that circumstance cuts off rant at the source.

Sam, the youngest of the one-time crew of seven, is the only labor left, and I must admit that his solitude tempers my intensity. I ask myself, is it fair to require of Sam what you formerly demanded from his six collective siblings? And the answer is always no. There is little justification, even for a Simon Legree like me, for making Sam the final focus of my every effort to avoid yardwork. Even I can see that. So Sam is indulged, even spoiled a bit, and here it is mid-summer and I've still got half the spring chores to complete. Sometimes, on these soft August mornings, I look around and wonder if the place isn't going to go to hell completely. I mean, look at those weeds in the strawberries; and how many times have I told myself I would fill in that canyoned rut in the driveway.

Looking back (and looking ahead, which is dismal indeed) I begin to wonder if any of the Zero Population Growth folks have ever lived in the country. I can easily understand, the prices of apartments being what they are, why city families might choose to limit the number of offspring. After all, there's only so much space in three rooms, even with a convertible sofa bed. And what's there to do with a six-footer who needs exercise when you're on the fifteenth floor.

Send him to the country, that's what. I can use him. The way things have gone (or haven't gone) this summer, I can see that I should have done my best to increase our built-in labor force. We never should have stopped at seven. Holy mackerel, I'm just now getting around to patching up the barn roof, and that job should have been done in June. I doubt if I'll ever get trimming the tall grass along the drive, and as far as painting the dory goes—forget it. Without my crew, it's all I can do to keep the lawn mowed.

It's enough to make a fellow yearn for winter.

CITYSIDE / COPING

The Whoomper Factor

As THIS is being written, snow is falling in the streets of Boston in what weather forecasters like to call "record amounts." I would guess by looking out the window that we are only a few hours from that magic moment of paralysis, as in *Storm Paralyzes Hub.* Perhaps we are even due for an *Entire Region Engulfed* or a *Northeast Blanketed,* but I will happily settle for mere local disablement. And the more the merrier.

Some people call them blizzards, other nor'easters. My own term is whoompers, and I freely admit looking forward to them as does a baseball fan to April. Usually I am disappointed, however, because tonight's storm warnings too often turn into tomorrow's light flurries.

Well, flurries be damned. I want the real thing, complete with Volkswagens turned into drifts along Commonwealth avenue and the MBTA's third rail frozen like a hunk of raw meat. A storm does not even begin to qualify as a whoomper unless Logan Airport is shut down for a minimum of six hours.

The point is, whoompers teach us a lesson. Or rather several lessons. For one thing, here are all these city folk who pride themselves on their instinct for survival, and suddenly they cannot bear to venture into the streets because they are afraid of being swallowed up. Virtual prisoners in their own houses is what they are. In northern New England, the natives view nights such as this with casual indifference, but let a whoomper hit Boston and the locals are not only knee deep in snow but also in befuddlement and disarray.

The lesson? That there is something more powerful out there than the sacred metropolis. It is not unlike the message we can read into the debacle of the windows falling out of the John Hancock Tower: just when we think we've got the upper hand on the elements, we find out we are flies and someone else is holding the swatter. Whoompers keep us in our place.

They also slow us down, which is not a bad thing for urbania these days. Frankly, I'm of the opinion Logan should be closed periodically, snow or not, in tribute to the lurking suspicion that it may not be all that necessary for a man to travel at a speed of 600 miles per hour. In a little while I shall go forth into the streets and I know what I will find. People will actually be *walking,* and the avenues will be bereft of cars. It will be something like those marvelous photographs of Back Bay during the nineteenth century, wherein the lack of clutter and traffic makes it seem as if someone has selectively airbrushed the scene.

And, of course, there will be the sound of silence tonight. It will be almost deafening. I know city people who have trouble sleeping in the country because of the lack of noise, and I suspect this is what bothers many of them about whoompers. Icy sidewalks and even fewer parking spaces we can handle, but please, God, turn up the volume. City folks tend not to believe in anything they can't hear with their own ears.

It should also be noted that nights such as this are obviously quite pretty, hiding the city's wounds beneath a clean white dressing. But it is their effect on the way people suddenly treat each other that is most fascinating, coming as it does when city dwellers are depicted as people of the same general variety as those New Yorkers who stood by when Kitty Genovese was murdered back in 1964.

There's nothing like a good whoomper to get people thinking that everyone walking towards them on the sidewalk might not be a mugger, or that saying hello is not necessarily a sign of perversion. You would think that city people, more than any other, would have a strong sense of being in the same rough seas together, yet it is not until a quasi catastrophe hits that many of them stop being lone sharks.

But enough of this. There's a whoomper outside tonight, and it requires my presence.

COUNTRYSIDE / COPING

Spring Painting

ANY GOOD country housepainter will tell you that September is the best time of the year to give the exterior of your home a fresh coat of paint. By then, if the weather has been halfway decent, the hot suns of summer will have dried out most of the moisture in the wood; with a clapboard house especially, there is less chance the paint will pop, blister, or peel a few weeks after it goes on. I learned that lesson while I worked as a housepainter—a job I took on in the years I was a commercial fisherman. Painting was a good fill-in when the weather kept us ashore, or the winter winds blew too icily for me.

But no matter how many times I gave the autumnal word to customers, or how many times I repeated the advice to myself, spring was always a painter's busiest season. About this time of the year, as mid-April turned the corner, I would get more calls than I could handle. Someone had a garage here, a fence there, a sunporch or a kitchen they wanted freshened with a new coat of paint, or two, or even three. By then, I was reluctant to make such commitments; the best of the fishing was on its way and I didn't want to get caught with a brush in my hand when I ought to be setting a net offshore.

Even so, I've never yet learned how to say no, and those Aprils always found me painting like a madman, trying to get caught up so I would be free to run for the dory whenever the word went out that the fish had arrived. For a fellow who was once nicknamed "Awky" by his teammates, who held their breath every time I had to field a fly ball in rightfield, I often surprised myself with the speed and competence of my painting. Over the years, I actually acquired a measure of skill.

For me, that was something to be proud of. The first time I ever laid brush on wood was when I was a boy and had built what amounted to a box that was to become a rabbit hutch. I wanted it white, and I found a can of paint in the barn along with a brush in fair condition. I slapped the paint on late in a summer afternoon, then went in for supper. When I came out in the long twilight to check on my work, the hutch was gray, not white. So many mosquitoes, flies, and fuzzbills had stuck in the wet paint that they ruined the entire job. As a bonus, the brush (which my father had once carefully cleaned and put away) was stiff with clotted paint. I heard about that the next morning.

That was the start of my education in painting. I had some fine teachers; I learned how to mix colors, how to clean brushes, how to scrape and sand, how to work indoors and out. The best part of my training came on April weekends like this one when I was in my early teens, a schoolboy, home on Saturday and Sunday. Almost every year, my mother would ask me to paint the trim on some part of the house, or the barn/garage. It was a chore I never turned down.

We lived in a wonderful spot then; the house was near the end of a narrow neck of land between the ocean and a salt pond. Up on the ladder on a sunny April morning, I could hear the surf rolling and thumping along the beach just over the dunes, and if I climbed high enough, up to the wooden fake chimney on the roof that had to be painted, I could look out over the entire pond where flocks of sheldrake in their bright spring plumage played their mating games with splashings, flutterings and much commotion on the dappled waters.

Sometimes, in the afternoon, when the wind came 'round southwest, I could hear geese calling far out over the open ocean. Then I would lie flat on my back on the roof, still as a post. If I was lucky, the wavering lines of Canada geese would appear over the dunes, flying low, talking back and forth, ready to land in the pond for their annual layover on the flight north. There were many times when they failed to spot me and soared, it seemed then, just a few feet overhead; I could see their feathers, feet, and eyes, and their calling sounded loud in my ears.

One still, windless morning when the pond stretched like a silken scarf, I sat on the chimney and watched for hours as a half-dozen ospreys dove on a school of alewives that had entered the pond from the ocean. The hawks would fall, wings folded, into the still water, and a plume of spray would hang there in the sun.

Which is why I have a wooden boat that needs painting each April. Every time I open a can and smell fresh paint, I am back on that roof, watching geese fly and ospreys dive.

Boston's Vertical Mile

THERE ONCE was a time, back in our innocence or something, when March supposedly signaled windy times. That was before skyscrapers, of course. Now the windy season lasts 365 days a year in Boston, hurtling its way down glass and steel tunnels with only minor assistance from nature. Woe be to the poor soul strolling along Federal street who, while walking beneath the First National Bank Building, decides to open his or her raincoat. (Flashers beware.) The last time I witnessed such an incident (which didn't happen to involve a flasher), a full-sized human male was lifted an inch or so off the ground. The terrified look on his face indicated that he was not particularly enamored with being transformed into a kite.

There is no record of anyone being blown away in Boston, but give them time. *Them* in this case being the Boston Redevelopment Authority and other interested parties who in recent years have had a hand in turning this city into a place only Superman could love. Oh, there is a lot of official talk about finally building "people amenities" now that we've papered the sky with concrete. But that seems a little like calling the doctor after the undertaker has finished his work.

As for the patient, Boston came down with high-rise fever on April 19, 1965. That was the day the Prudential Center was dedicated, therby transforming 31¼ acres of unattractive railroad yards into fifty-two floors of unattractive non-architecture. But even if a 750-foot Venus deMilo had been constructed on the spot, it, too, would probably have brought the high winds and vast numbers of people that have made the Boylston street area the Hub's own little combination of Mt. Washington and Times Square.

Like so many overgrown wooden Indians, downtown replicas soon followed the Pru's pointy lead. The State Street Bank Building checked in at thirty-four stories, New England Merchants at forty, the First National at thirty-seven. The Boston Company Building added forty-one more floors, One Beacon Street chipped in with forty, the Shawmut Bank tossed in thirty-eight, and sixty State Street added thirty-eight for good measure. All this, of course, only leads straight back to the Back Bay, where the John Hancock Tower has reportedly been exorcised of its paneful dilemma and is about to open its sixty-story rhomboid shape to one and all. What the decade adds up to is roughly a vertical mile of office space. Boston, which a century ago so industriously built itself *out,* is now totally built *up.*

I just wish someone could convince me that we really need these things. Tell me why they must loom so outrageously over the waterfront, emit so many people into Copley Square and generally destroy the gentle roll of the city as viewed from across the Charles.

A couple of years ago, while journalistically attempting to sort out the infamous Hancock glass caper, I'm afraid I may have made a startling discovery about skyscrapers: there seems to be as much known about building them as there is about Howard Hughes. At first I thought I was being conned, that everyone from architects to construction workers was clamming up out of mortal fear. After a while, I realized they knew as little as they pretended. Maybe less.

The thing is, putting up a skyscraper isn't like making a car. You can't run a test model around the track. You can't practice. You can't throw the bad ones away. You just sort of put it up, and if it works, fine. If it doesn't, well, son of a gun. Sure, you can run a few laboratory tests, but several judges and juries are about to spend the next few years dealing with the question of just how well such precautions worked in l'affaire Hancock. Answer: not very. As a result, Back Bay is now the proud home of a 790-foot glass test tube. Downtown Boston, meanwhile, is a collection of giant beakers.

Hold onto your hat. And button up your overcoat.

A Mean Cat for a Tough Job

"DON'T YOU miss having neighbors?" is a question many visitors ask when they reach our home. Coming from suburban settlements where people are as close as a shared sneeze, our visitors are often discomfited by the apparent isolation of our place. Shorn of their accustomed lawn-to-lawn environments, the travelers seem almost afraid of the woods that border our lawn, as if aliens were hiding there, behind the oaks and spruce.

When I answer the question, I usually reply that we don't miss the clatter of adjoining garbage cans, and let it go at that. I don't talk much about the neighbors we do have. Ignorance is bliss, the line goes, so I allow our visitors to depart without ever giving them the details about the creatures with whom we share our real estate.

If I told the truth about red squirrels, gray squirrels, deer mice, moles, voles, fishers and ferrets, I might truly frighten the friendly folks who have come calling. I myself never imagined the host of neighbors we would entertain; but almost before the house was finished, they came to visit, dropping by, as good neighbors should, to leave a small token of proper welcome. Red squirrels left holes in the eaves, seeds on the shelves, and puffs of insulating material on the breakfast table to let us know they had watched over us during the night. Gray squirrels ate the sunflower seed put out for the birds, voles and moles wreaked havoc on the bulbs we had so carefully carried from our former homestead. Deer mice became most neighborly during the winter; their symmetrical droppings and properly feathered nests (feathers courtesy of a gnawed sofa cushion) turned up almost everywhere.

It got so I wondered what our two cats were doing with their spare time. After all, I said to the cat keeper, isn't rodent control the reason why we feed these louts? I was on the point of drop-kicking the feline pair (languid mother and worthless son) across

108

the bay when they each disappeared, within a week or so of each other.

"Fisher got 'em," said my good friend and experienced woodsman, Arthur Hummer. And, indeed, based on some fast research and observation, it became clear that Arthur was right. Fishers, those overgrown combinations of wolverines and weasels so beloved for their expensive pelts, have made a comeback in Maine. Having eaten every porcupine on our place (and there were scores) they demolished the two cats before moving on to other slaughters.

Why don't fishers eat red squirrels, gray squirrels, moles, voles and deer mice? I asked no one in particular, and set about pondering our problem. The neighbors were ruining the neighborhood.

I am some way into the solution, and have to admit it begins to look like a failure. My notion was to acquire a super-cat, a cat so mean it would not only mop up on the smaller rodents, but would rip the sod in search of moles and send fishers scurrying for the next county. Finding no one who could give me the genetic formula for utter viciousness, I began scouting for signs of meanness on my own.

Passing the window of Day's News and Variety one afternoon, I noticed Pete had put kittens (To Give Away) in the display area, and as I watched, I saw one cuff his siblings without mercy. That's my cat, I said, and took it home, handling it roughly all the way.

To get the kid started right, I named it Ghengis Khan Badass Attila and served him his first meal of gunpowder. That was several weeks ago. To this day he has done nothing meaner than moving from the sofa to the chair in front of the stove. When he goes outdoors, he pushes pretty leaves around. A mole wandered up from below the roses and surfaced in front of Attila; the boy went back to his leaves.

This being the season (now that Thanksgiving is by) for gifts, I'm wondering if there is anyone out there who can tell me what to feed Attila so he grows up mean enough to tear the hide off an

109

alligator. Given the neighbors we have, we're going to need a cat like that, and soon.

The Joy of Decks

SPRING IS a wonderful time of year in the city. Forget the myth that urban folks don't notice the change of seasons. Of course we do. An automobile owner living in Boston can sniff a winter storm before the most grizzled of rural veterans. And the first warm day in April turns the Esplanade, Castle Island, and other patches of greenery into bright blizzards of pale bodies paying holy if premature homage to the sun.

April is also the month which sparks that inner city elitist known as the roof deck owner. Creating his or her own human version of Ground Hog Day, this urban strategist carefully tests the conditions before emerging from the cocoon as a butterfly for six or seven months. Meanwhile, all persons not enjoying the pleasures of a rooftop hideaway are viewed by this creature as living the drab lives of moths.

But that's Deck Culture for you. It is a lot like Yard Culture, but on a higher plane. After all, almost everyone out there in the suburbs has a yard; but a roof deck in the middle of Boston is a status symbol akin only to owning one's own private parking space. (On second thought, nothing is akin to owning your own parking space.)

What grass is to the suburbanite, planking is to the deckite. It is turf. Title. Estate. This time of year, Deck Culture means greeting each other warmly across roofs which act as electrified fences. The camaraderie of the well-stationed abounds, but there is also the knowledge that there is a certain amount of competition ahead. Keeping up with the Joneses' wrought iron is not to be taken too lightly. Still, there are simply no two decks alike (unless you include those cookie-cutter balconies hanging from high-rise apartments, which you shouldn't), so rivalry is minimized. Does a Bentley owner envy the possessor of a Rolls?

Deck Culture includes much of the tomfoolery and tackiness of Yard Culture. Barbecues, for example. And "lawn" furniture. What turns life on a rooftop into a figurative high as well as a literal one is the firm belief that the laws of nature have been beaten. God, the feeling goes, did not intend people to live in the city *and* eat charcoaled hamburgers. Nor did He intend people to acquire suntans there. (For that is why He created smog, right?) Deck Culture, then, is a kind of mystical power trip, a sort of shaking your fist skyward and shouting, "See? See? I can have my steak and eat it, too!"

The deck gives you the illusion of privacy in an open environment. People do things on their roofs that they wouldn't dare do in front of other people, even though dozens of windows are leering up and down at them. From my own roof I have observed deck activity ranging from a wedding to nude sunbathing. And while I have never partaken in either activity on my deck, I have done a few things which have later caused me to reevaluate my sense of seclusion.

If the penultimate in Deck Culture is sleeping on the roof, then the ultimate is making love up there. Or maybe it's the other way around. In any case, it is tricky business. Not only is it *de rigueur* to wait until sundown, but it should be noted that there are backdrops more romantic than the gentle sway of office buildings. On the other hand, there is nothing quite like being awakened by the soft chirping of automobile horns or rising to see the morning sun reflected in the John Hancock Tower. That's urban Deck Culture for you, and where can you find anything like it in the suburbs?

Sustaining Green

PUT YOURSELF atop a ridge, looking down into a green and rolling valley, or on a point taking in a vista that sweeps across the bay and on to a panorama of verdant meadows and towering trees. Asked for an opinion, you are most likely to put it simply and say, "It's beautiful." Like me, and hundreds of millions of beings, you instinctively find beauty in the elementary pageantry of nature—trees, grass, woods, meadows and the green of growing things.

I wonder occasionally how deep the roots of beauty reach. I surmise, for example, that forests and meadows and flowers are indisputably lovely because we have learned over the millennia that green is the color of our survival. Without photosynthesis, without the incredible work plants do to purify our air, provide us with oxygen for our lungs, water for our world and sustenance for our suppers, humankind would perish instantly from this planet. The green in our view is vital; it is essential to every life cycle.

That's why a voice within us sings when our eyes sweep from a ridge or across a bay; it is telling us that green is good, that its presence is part of a mighty design. The opposite is also true. No matter now urban our culture, there is a tremor whenever open land is devoured by machines. No human sits easily as witness to the gouging of a meadow, the felling of a forest or the asphalt suffocation of the sod. There are too many eons of experience that shout warnings against such callous treatment of the life source.

Lest we forget, even in the long winters of this Yankee land, we have been granted some green to sustain us through the deepest snows and the most bitter cold. Long after the leaves have left the trees and frost has furled the fields, after the harvest is complete and the bay is silenced, the evergreens of our world stand as reminders of the growing seasons.

I can not imagine how these New England winters could be endured without the pine, the spruce and fir. Consider this landscape without them. There would be no shred of life in it. Above you the bare, brown branches of oak, maple, chestnut and elm; along the roads the sere stretches of nondescript shrubs poking above the snow's deserts—that's what you would see. The entire environment would be a testimony to the drab; you could find no hope in your world.

But we are saved by the conifers. There is scarcely a stretch of space from Vermont to Maine and south past the Cape where some evergreen or other has not taken stubborn root. In the vast woodlands to the north, their reaches run for scores of miles— great green seas whitecapped with crowns of snow, trembling in the winter winds. In towns like mine, grown so quickly in just decades, the evergreens persist. Pasture pine grows where farms once were; firs tumble along the banks at the edge of the sea; proud blue spruce stand tall at the center of the town's memorials, planted there by men who understood their constant dignity.

These evergreens make a mockery of December. Their limbs are lush, they swing with life as we walk through the woods. Even their fragrance prevails. Like the perfume of a summer's blossom, the pungence of a balsam pervades the frigid air—a sweet statement of defiance to the storms that thought themselves the conquerors of these lands. Even the ice can not long humble the evergreen. Bent by it after a night of sleet, the green boughs refuse to break. They wait for the wind and sun to join and then spring free, flinging frozen crystals in the cold air as a horse might toss its mane.

We have a natural reverence for these trees. Something there is in their spirit that reaches deep in humankind. Two-hundred years ago, the white pine's green became the standard of the first flags of the Revolution; it still marks the standard of the State of

Maine. We are drawn to these great trees, I believe, because they are such a sturdy symbol of the life-force in every growing forest and field. The evergreens keep that voice singing within us when the rest of this world surrenders to the snows.

And that's why, I believe, we bring evergreen garlands and wreathes and trees into our homes at this season and for these holidays. The impulse goes beyond "decoration," beyond even tradition and rites we may grant to other cultures. It goes back to the central and fundamental recognition that these boughs and trees and wreathes stand at the center of our life support system, the crux of the mighty design.

That's why we say, "It's beautiful," when we see the first wreath on the door, or smell the balsam in the room. And that's why we know such gratitude when we travel this northern land and see the evergreens nod as we go by.

Into Everyone's Life a Little B and E Must Fall

MY FRIEND Harold was clearly perturbed. He was sweeping up wood shavings around his front door when I saw him, separating them into two neat little piles. "These were made by the locksmith," he said, nodding toward one of the mounds. "And these," he added solemnly, turning to the other accumulation, "these were made by the burglar."

Bad news for Harold when he had arrived home from work that day: breaking and entering. B&E, in the vernacular. By Person/s Unk. Nothing serious, mind you, just your standard junkie-in-search-of-color-TV-and-cash type of thing. The apartment lock had been jimmied with your standard crowbar, but this particular Person Unk. had also demonstrated a certain flair. According to witnesses (who included an apparently nonchalant meter maid), he had arrived in a taxi and departed in another. "He must have known that you can never find a parking space around here," mused Harold. The fellow had also left two new screwdrivers behind, still wrapped in the brown bag in which they had been purchased. "Probably stopped to pick them up on the way," Harold theorized. "Hope they work better than the TV did."

But of course, Harold wasn't laughing. He'd been hit, as they say. The uniformed police, polite but unconcerned, had come and gone. Two detectives had put in an appearance. "We should check with the boys in Station One," one of them had told the other. "*We're* from Station One," his partner replied.

The television set had been traced to an appliance store, where police reported they "lost" it. And now Harold was busily cleaning up after workmen who had installed two new heavy duty bolt locks of intimidating proportions, a chain lock apparently forged out of Kryptonite, and an alarm system guaranteed to make grown men quiver. "I thought this would look like Fort Knox when I finished, but it looks worse," he lamented. "It looks like New York."

Cheer up, I told Harold. You've lived in Boston eleven years and this is the first time you've been hit. Ask any suburbanite, and he or she will gladly tell you that no one can live in the city for eleven years without getting strangled, let alone burglarized. They know because they read the papers. And because a friend's cousin's sister's former husband once had his pocket picked in Park Street station.

"That's the point," Harold answered, sweeping his shavings into a dustpan. "I know people in the suburbs who get hit about once a year. Out there the burglars don't show up in cabs; they come in vans. Whole rooms disappear at once. Those people sit around and say, 'It can't happen here,' and meanwhile somebody's rifling the pantry for the silverware. Well, that's the way I was. I figured I was above it all. It was nice. Now I'm paranoid. I'm carrying around more keys than a jailer. I don't like it."

Everything has a price, I reminded him. Lots of people don't spend their early evenings relaxing like you do; they spend them taking long breathers on the Southeast Expressway. Their idea of going to the theater is sitting down to watch "Upstairs Downstairs." They eat in shopping center restaurants which serve those combinations of steak and lobster.

"Damned junkies," Harold continued to mutter.

Damned junkies is right, I agreed. As the courts sometimes like to say about certain similar obscenities, they have no redeeming social value. But what are you going to do, Harold? Move out? There are junkies in the suburbs, too. Turn your apartment into your own little version of M.C.I. Walpole if you must, but don't give up the urban ship over somebody with a crowbar and cab fare. Love/hate is what living in Boston is all about. For every Green Line there's an Esplanade. For every city assessor there's a quirky hideaway. For every pothole there's . . . there's . . .

"Gotcha there," Harold said.

Just remember, I told him, that into everyone's life a little B&E must fall.

COUNTRYSIDE / COPING

The Stoveside Napper

THE OIL squeeze, I have learned on these mid-winter days in the country, has some advantages. Like most Downeasters—the eighty percent whose homes (statisticians tell us) are heated by oil—I was properly alarmed by the autumnal headlines shouting the unwelcome news that home heating oil would cost more than fifty cents a gallon. It was enough to stir me into getting my wood in before the first snowflake drifted past our windowpane. It was also enough to send Peter Cox, landlord of the old house where the *Maine Times* office is located, into a conservation swivel.

He has not yet allowed one drop of petro-fuel to be pumped into what once was a tank for heating oil in the cellar. Instead, those of us who share space in this rambling and graceful former sea captain's mansion must lug logs and split kindling if we are to survive this region's customary climatic chill. The solitary nature of my occupation (writing has seldom been otherwise) means that I share my office space with a small ship's stove. My room is difficult to find; tucked away in an upstairs corner, it is, by choice and design, a place of quiet privacy, highly unlikely to be discovered by any walk-in clients.

I travel here from my home in the morning, and start, or revive, stoves in both places; when I leave my office in the evening, I return to an easy chair (and other accoutrements of relaxation) as close as safety will permit to the primary stove of our home. My January life, if you will, can be measured in the distance likely to be found between myself and the nearest mass of warm cast-iron.

Somewhere in the course of my desultory reading on wood, wood stoves, and other post-petroleum heating systems, I discovered that the molecular nature of heat from a piping metal stove is more friendly than most. It has the distinct advantage of making a body feel warmer because of the kind of heat that is generated and the way it is transmitted through the atmosphere, clothing and the human skin. I had always felt that no system ever seemed as warm as a good, hot stove; my reading gave me scientific confirmation of my senses.

Which is why, I keep telling myself, I have taken to napping so frequently. Oh, part of this latest effort of mine to stay in top physical and mental condition has, I am certain, to do with January and the knowledge that this is, after all, a somnolent time of the year, hung as it is between the zest of autumn and the excitement of approaching spring. But it also has to do with stoves.

I return to the office after a light lunch—nothing more than a cheese soufflé, a glass or two of Montrachet, some coffee ice cream and a macaroon—and no sooner am I settled in my swivel chair, poised like a shrike before my typewriter, but I am o'ertaken by this compulsion to relax, to lean back in the chair, to rest the back of my head against the top of the chair-back, to lift my feet to the low bookcase nearby and then to close my eyes. When I do that in the circle of contented warmth radiated by a castiron stove, I enter another world: the world of nap.

When he napped, Hemingway's Old Man (of "The Old Man and the Sea") dreamt of lions on the beach. We each have our different styles; when I nap, the warm void is dreamless. I drift through time as easily as a schooner moving with the tide. Fifteen or twenty minutes later, my easy journey ends, my eyes open, my feet move back to the floor, my head lifts, and I approach my work with an energy previously unknown, all the while charged with gratitude for the oil squeeze and the wood stoves it has brought into my life.

I find the napping experience so captivating a restorative that I may repeat the routine at home, in the evening. Over the weeks, my conditioning has improved until I can often nap two or three times in the same day, without shortness of breath, or muscle cramps. So enjoyable is the experience that I want to share it. I would like to see a nation of nappers, and I feel for those millions denied the privacy of a solitary office like mine. Unlike the joggers who take to the streets so full of self-righteous self-discipline that no boss would think of reprimanding them for time away from work, a napper is likely to get fired on the first nod.

That is an injustice of the gravest sort which must soon be set to rights. Thus I say thank goodness for the oil squeeze which is doing so much to make wood stoves and naps fashionable again.

Tennis and the Common Man

LORD KNOWS tennis was never intended to be an urban game. In 1874, the modern version of the sport made its way from the English countryside to Bermuda to Staten Island, neglecting to stop in any cities along the way. Things haven't changed much. Despite hyperbolic claims to the contrary, tennis has not been "democratized" to the point that "everybody" plays.

When Humphrey Bogart first asked "Tennis anyone," uttering the question as a minor line in a minor play in 1922, he was merely wondering aloud if just *anyone* should be allowed to play. Tennis is still a genteel and suburban game, even though it takes up no more space than basketball. Now *there's* a city game, and the implications of the contrast in urban popularity between the two sports are clear: the whiteness of tennis is not limited to clothing.

Despite all this (or perhaps even because of it), playing tennis on public courts in downtown Boston is high adventure. Actually, playing anywhere for free in the city is a bit speculative, since only seventy-two courts are municipally owned. That's one for approximately every 8900 residents, and even a novice knows that playing 4450 to a side is a bit stifling.

Newton, a city approximately one-seventh as large as Boston, has but thirteen fewer public courts. And only two of the Hub's, those on Boston Common, are located in what you could really call the "downtown" area. Further, one of these courts requires a permit to play, the theory apparently being that to throw both of them open on a first-come, first-serve basis would leave them in control of the Amboy Dukes or some other party which might not look too fondly on dispossession.

Oh, the incongruity of it all! Playing tennis on something called "Common!" A whole new terminology! ("Lobbing into the sun" is now "Lobbing into the Hancock.") No one will ever mistake these two green Grass-Tex hard surfaces for the comfortable red clay

119

to be found in the stadium at Longwood. But there the dissimilarities do not end.

Very early on a recent Sunday morning, so early that many members of Longwood probably were still enjoying Saturday, a foursome on the Common consisted of a black, a Filipino, a left-handed woman and a WASPish looking young gentleman who must have taken a wrong turn on the way to Wellesley. The ping of the ball was drowned out by the shouts from the neighboring softball field, where the Lite-guzzling "BPDs" were thumping the Schlitz out of the "C&Ds." The tennis players did not appear to notice the revelry, so earnestly were they on the lookout for the soft-drink cans which have caused more than one nasty spill on the Common courts.

But that's the fun of it. Where else can you hit a delicate drop shot and know that a gallery of sage winos will rattle their paper bags in appreciation? Where else can you scurry along the baseline only to screech to a halt as you realize that it has been appropriated by a practitioner of yoga? Where else can you wander onto a court and be warmly welcomed into a game by an urchin who informs you that your presence will make the teams even—nine against nine.

But make no mistake about it. Some of these people can *play*. Your topspin backhand would be deadly, too, if you'd developed it as a weapon to drive your opponents toward a ten-speed bike which has been known to materialize in the backcourt. The Common player has an instinct for survival which is horrendously difficult to overcome. He is a devilish craftsman who has had to work so hard to get his court and to hang onto it that he is not about to insult his commitment by losing.

I once was pitted against a wily veteran who so measured his shots that he repeatedly could put them through the holes at the top of the net without causing so much as an observable flicker. If that didn't work he called upon a slice serve calculated to send me toppling over the players who were waiting for our hour to end like a group of prospective heirs expecting to take over the estate.

Now *he* was the type of Common character who shouldn't be allowed to play the game.

The Island Graveyard

By NOVEMBER, hundreds of Maine's islands have been deserted. The scores of patches and hummocks that perch like birds on the gray sea are braced for their lonely Decembers; the children of summer have gone, sloops and yawls no longer slip around the points and into quiet coves. Cottage doors are shut tight and no hands but the wind's shall tug at them until Decoration Day.

A century ago, even in mid-November, there were no such departures. The islands then were home, not places of seasonal pleasure. Then it was the mainland that seemed so formidable. The waterways were the fairest of roads, the islands the most accessible of lands, the surrounding sea the most fertile of farms. Alongside clearings cut by settlers of yet an earlier time—who saw the islands as sanctuaries from soldiers and savages—families of the Nineteenth Century lived year-round in island communities that stretched the length of the Main coast, scattered as if they had been thrown to the winds from atop some mainland cliff.

The marks of those settlements are on the islands still. Gravestones and evergreens stand together where once a churchyard was. The woods have returned to reclaim the land those islanders had sanctified with the burials of their elders and their children.

Such discoveries are difficult to put aside. I walked an island recently; thinking myself an explorer of a wild and unwalked place, I thrilled at the notion that where I stepped only wild creatures and wild Indians had trod before. Then I came upon the graveyard gate, still hung from its hand-hammered hinges on

121

a cedar post and I found the small, sad headstones of children's graves, the engraved and flowery messages of devotion on the grave markers of wives and mothers next to the high monuments in memory of the sea captains and farmers who had once built a village where I stood in ignorance of their achievements.

In clear patches that had once been fields, gnarled apple trees have lasted longer than those who planted them and tasted their first fruits. And near the trees are the cellar holes of the islanders' houses, built from the spruce and pine and oak that had never known an axe until the settlers came. Some fields are still cleared, their centers marked by great piles of stone.

The smaller stones, I have been told, were carried by the children; the middling round rocks heaved up by the women, and the large boulders towed by laboring men and oxen. Each one of the thousands in these island mounds was carried or pulled from the ground before the plow could endure and seed take root.

The rock piles are as high as my head; they cover a full half-acre of ground. It is not possible, I tell myself, that men and women and children picked and hauled and stooped and carried every one of the stones to this place with their hands alone. But it is so, and the work was done after the patch of ground had been cleared of trees with hand axes and hand saws, the stumps pulled by men and oxen. Then the stones were picked and the boulders pulled; then the plow was pushed, the thin soil turned and crops planted.

Without that harvest by this time in November, the islanders could not survive till spring. By these gray days of the darkening year, those islanders had to have done their work or die. In weeks, the few pastures there would be snowbound; the stock had to have enough hay and corn; the cows had to be fed enough to give milk for the island's children. Root cellars had to be stocked with potatoes; dried apples had to be stored, venison cut, fish salted and beef cured. By mid-November it was known there could be no surcease from the freezing sea, no passage made across the icy straits.

122

Like passengers on a ship adrift in the open sea, those islanders of 100 years ago had only each other and the fruits of their labors to carry them from their Novembers to their Mays. What a purification and suffering their winters must have been. Their days and nights were carried like the rocks from the fields, each one an effort, each one counted alongside the food still left.

Compared to those whose gravestones still stand among the island evergreens, we know nothing of November. For us it requires merely a tightening of hope along with a tightening of our mufflers. For us it is complaints of gray even as we contemplate the holidays to come. For us, this month in New England is merely an interlude and proof that winter is indeed on its way. We have come to complain about Novembers here, as if we are due something better.

I have a cure for such complaints. It is out there on any of those hundreds of Maine islands that have been deserted by the soft voices of summer and left to face their Decembers alone, except for the memories and the markers of those island folk who once turned to face their own winters together.

CITYSIDE / COPING

Fair Weather Friends

WE'RE IN the thick of it now. Winter has descended upon the town in earnest, and those who can afford the tariff are beseeching travel agents for passage to any place with a temperature above freezing. ("How about Waco, Texas, sir?" *"Gimme the ticket!"*) As for most of the rest of us, we've hunkered down with whatever or whomever keeps us warm, dreaming fond dreams of steamy Fourth of July traffic jams.

If we lived in the country, of course, we would be experiencing no visible discomfort. As Norman Rockwell and the pictures on insurance company calendars repeatedly make clear, winter is a perfectly acceptable item in rural New England. The same people who shiver and shake when the temperature in downtown Boston dips into the teens feel positively invigorated by standing in Bread Loaf, Vt., with the mercury at thirty below. Winter is considered a healthy state of affairs if experienced in the country, where the snow wouldn't dare get dirty. In the city, people hasten to tell you, it actually falls to earth in the form of cinders.

The whole thing is just one more reason for urbania to hire a public relations agent. What we need is someone to tell the world that city life doesn't necessarily cease after the first day in December. This is a thankless bit of work, one that is destined to bring snide retorts even from one's own urban neighbors. It takes a great deal of courage to stand up to the people who make calendars for insurance companies.

It does no good to tell people that skating and sledding exist only a few hundred yards from one's city door. (Skiing, one admits, *is* an exclusively rural activity, and country folks are welcome to all the lift lines they desire.) Or that it is possible to take long walks virtually alone through a city snowstorm, enjoying the unexpected silence and sudden paralysis that grinds man's newest machines to a halt. No, outsiders have already decided that the only things worth seeing in Boston during the winter are the Christmas lights on the Common during December and the return counters of the department stores in January.

In the meantime, they paint their fanciful pictures of upcountry romance: log fires, sleigh rides, and kids bundling into snowsuits. Now I do not claim to be an expert on surviving winter in New England's northern parts, but I do know that "surviving" is not a bad word choice for the activity. I also know that no cases of cabin fever have ever been reported in Dorchester or Jamaica Plain.

You want log fires? Good, because you will need plenty of them when it snows for four consecutive days and you are living on the fifth dirt road off the paved road which leads to the main road which connects to the highway. And sleigh rides? Just the thing when the plow hasn't come up to clear your road in more than a month and it looks as if it won't get through to you until spring. Snowsuits? It is reliably reported that the typical northern New England child is zipped into winter clothing in November and released with a whoosh in April. That may be Norman Rockwell's idea of a winter wonderland, but it is not mine.

But perhaps it's just as well that the myths persist. During the winter, Boston can cleanse its pores of tourists and other part-timers. Let them have their ski slopes and their six-foot drifts and their cars in snowbanks by the side of the road. That way the rest of us can spend winter in hibernation, secure in the knowledge that when the temperatures rise in the spring we will be awakened by the onrushing clatter of thousands of invaders who can literally be called fair weather friends.

COUNTRYSIDE / COPING

Wind

OUR MOST unwelcome visitors have returned. They come silently, invisible, yet they are a presence as persistently disagreeable as a toothache, as discomforting as a long overdue bill. I speak of the cold winds of the season; the gales of approaching November, the icy tumults of December. Like eels slipping sinuously through the smallest openings in the weavings of a fishing basket, the cold winds seek and find the joinings at every corner, every window, every roofline, every door, frame of the house. They enter in spite of their unwelcome.

I can feel their approach along the floor. Serpents that they are, the cold winds crawl from the north corner of the room to coil about my ankles, even as I seek to stir the fire. What, now, can I do to protect this place from this soundless invasion?

I marvel at what we have done. Over the past six years, we must have squeezed a half-ton of caulking into the slim avenues on which the wind walks in. Roger has popped some witches brew of solidifying foam into a hole the red squirrel chewed at the beam end where the roof rises over the living room. That hole is blocked, I know. The hardened foam protrudes like cooled lava—a signal to all future squirrels that this place is defended.

We go into the woods early every October to trim bottom branches from the balsam and hemlock. Load after load is pulled to the house and branches are laid as carefully as mason's bricks in an interwoven, evergreen banking that rims the house like a wreath where ground and shingles meet—yet another moat to trap the winds that would enter uninvited. And last year our neighbor, Alan, constructed and installed wooden shields that enclose the porch; what is a light and airy place in summer now becomes dark and confined—again, the sacrifice is made to baffle the winds.

When the sou'westers blow off the water, they send patrols to probe our weakest walls—the ones that corner the sleeping loft that has always been called Darragh's room, even though she has had a home of her own for several years. If I stand under the loft opening, I can feel the cold winds running like water down the wall. I have lost count of the times I have climbed the ladder to those battlements in vain attempts to find the traitorous joining that gives the winds free passage.

We seal the cellar entrance with long strips of silver duct tape, likewise the north-side vents that keep us cool in summer. The entire structure will meet November as armored as any knight of old, and equally as cumbersome. And, this year, we will find yet another weakness we have not discovered before; that, too, shall be caulked, or sealed, or stripped, or banked, or baffled, or just plain nailed shut.

But the winds are committed; they never surrender. We have slowed them, but our defense is far from iron-clad. Sometimes I wonder how many winters will have to pass, how many tons of caulking will have to be squeezed before we can claim victory. I'm not sure I shall ever mark that moment.

I have another plan. I want the wind to be tricked into working to defeat itself. My weapon is the windmill. Ideally, these wind dynamos would be small, low-cost, quiet, maintenance free, and they would generate electrical power which I would then send to space heaters built into the baseboards of the outermost rooms. As the winter winds blow, their defiant energy will be converted to the very prize they seek to rob us of: our warmth. I have fireside visions of hearing the winds howl with rage as they watch while their work sets the heating elements to glowing a cherry red. "Blow," I will say, "blow your hardest and be damned."

There are people working, I know, in Maine and in other parts of the nation to perfect just such windmills. Progress is difficult; wind generators are still in the vanguard of alternate energy systems. But given my actuarial years, I'm quite certain I shall live to see them perfected and sold as casually as woodstoves. When that happens, I shall be one of the first in line. Then, instead of gritting my teeth at the inevitable return of our most unwelcome visitors, I shall raise the windmill over the fortress of our home where it shall rise as a flashing banner proclaiming, at long last, our victory over winter's coldest winds.

CITYSIDE / COPING

Awaiting the Opener

IT WILL happen in eleven days, God and the Green Line willing. We will get off at Kenmore, press ourselves together in the rush to get up the stairs, and flow in great rivers toward the sixty-five-year-old structure in the distance. The turnpike will be traversed, the turnstyle confronted. And then it will be there in front of us: the field itself, looking so perfectly green as to suggest a color television picture gone irretrievably iridescent.

Up north the residents make note of spring's arrival by watching the creeks rise. Down here the seasonal change comes all at once, arriving promptly at 2 P.M. on a chosen day in April in the form of the first game at Fenway Park. Known simply, of course, as The Opener.

Ah, The Opener. For the rest of the long season the Red Sox will earn their title as "a New England team." Busloads of Kiwanis types will descend upon the park from the outlands, and suburban mothers will attempt to locate parking spaces while coping with station wagons filled with noisy adolescents. But The Opener is something else again. It is the rite—nay, the *right*—of city folks. Some of them are kids who wander over from Boston University to get high on dope in the bleachers, and many of them are guys who come in from Jamaica Plain to get high on Narragansett in Section 18. In any case, The Opener is our urban equinox, a crossing which in light of the winter just survived shall be marked a week from Thursday with considerable gusto, as it always is.

We always take several bottles of champagne. These are needed to help absorb the shock that sudden change frequently induces. For example, there was the unhappy year we discovered that the Pennant Grille, located on the corner of Brookline avenue and Landsdowne street when last we had looked, had been turned into a discotheque or something equally unsuitable during the off-season. The Pennant Grille! A bitter pill to swallow, leaving only the seedy Baseball Tavern as a suitable post-game round table. And there was last year's introduction to the new "instant replay" scoreboard in center field, a travesty perpetrated upon all of us by the small minds which have somehow gained control of the national pastime. But that is another column.

The Opener, you see, means more than simply eternal baseball optimism. It goes beyond blindly believing in the Olde Towne Team although it is being led by a man who actually lives in a place called Treasure Island, Florida, and whose qualifications

128

include a major league managing record of 156 wins and 224 losses. It transcends maintaining a stiff upper lip in the face of the fact the hated New York Yankees have purchased every decent player on earth who does not live in Cuba. And probably even some who do.

The Opener means everything is all right in the city again, despite the school buses, alleged charter reform, and a tax rate set by Scrooge McDuck. There is something wonderfully comforting in muttering "Same old Yaz" as No. 8 chops a two-hopper to the second baseman for the first of many times in a season. And this year the long-lost Boomer will return to draw raves for his fielding from some people who would do almost anything to prevent their kids from going to school with his.

Maybe it will rain. Perhaps it will even snow. It has done both during recent Openers, but no matter. We will bundle ourselves into the grandstand and take an occasional tug on our sustenance. Some of the people sitting around us will think George Scott is an actor, but that is also of little consequence. They are not really there for baseball. They are there because spring will officially arrive in the city at precisely 2 P.M. a week from Thursday. Or on whatever day the weather permits The Opener finally to be played.

COUNTRYSIDE / COPING

The Grapes Are on the Vine

THE GRAPES are on the vine. They are small and vividly green, too hard and bitter to attract even the most avaricious bird, but they are there, on their way to that autumnal maturity that has become a foreseeable certainty now that mid-July is upon us. I take note of their appearance because there was a time there back in the early days of May when I doubted that the young vines would survive the trauma of their pruning. I could see no hope for what seemed to be lifeless brown stalks which maintained that condition while the blossoming of the new spring went on all around them.

I questioned the Master Gardener. Not to worry, she said, dismissing my concern about what seemed a brutal pruning with the patronizing patience a scholar often displays toward a true ignoramus. She showed me small bumps on the stubs and claimed they were the beginnings of new growth that would soon be clambering up the sides of the arbor.

I had no choice. Either I could accept her decree or challenge it and then become obligated to learn something about the husbandry of Concords and perhaps something of the fundamentals of gardening in general. That I could not risk. It is my monumental ignorance (as carefully embellished over the years as any actor's favorite character) that has saved me from rake, hoe and pruning shear. I am kept out of both vegetable and flower garden because the fear of what my clumsy presence may ruin is greater than any desire to be relieved of weeding the strawberries or thinning the carrots. It is assumed by every member of the household (and it's an assumption I'm delighted to perpetuate) that I can not be left alone within hearing distance of a cultivated plant. Even the youngest in the family believes that I would rip up a lilac because I'm convinced it is poison ivy.

I am allowed to paint the boats, set the moorings, and, whenever the winds and the tides beckon, to go to sea alone in search of fresh seafood for the dinner table. If, as has often happened, I return empty-handed after eight hours of delight on the sparkling bay or the shores of a deserted island, there is only murmured complaint. Too strident a censure and I'm liable to be discouraged enough to try my hand at enhancing the corn—a risk to the greening stalks which the household is in no way prepared to bear.

But the grapes are on the vine, and as I make daily, discret checks on their progress I can see visions of my demise as a gardening ignoramus. There is something about the small green spheres and the knowledge of what they can become that tempts me to discard my finely wrought image as a botanical boob and take up hoe, rake and pruning shear with all the vigor I have known all along I could muster.

It is wine, of course, which lures me to squander the years invested in proclaiming seedling stupidity; I am prepared to gamble a decade of professed, and now credible, agricultural dumbness because I am finally convinced that wine does, indeed, come from grapes.

The process took a while. Nothing as delicious, as invigorating, as mysterious, as charming and as consistently surprising as wine could come from a bunch of grapes—that's what I believed for years. But knowledge is the enemy of absolutes, and as I continued to read the labels, I became persuaded.

I got quite convinced when I recently visited my only sister and her husband—a committed tinkerer with his farm and a fellow who now threatens to bring the Rothschilds to their knees with his vineyards in central Texas. After the dedicated consumption of the by-product of his grapes of former years, I knew in my heart I would never be satisfied with country life until I too could produce such pleasant beverages from my own home acres. It was a fateful moment which I have not made public until now.

But looking at the grapes on the vine this morning, I realized my days as a non-gardener are fast approaching their end. Hello, hoe.

CITYSIDE / COPING

Use and Overuse

WE ARE not so smart after all. Look how long it took us to understand what John Sears, then-commissioner of the Metropolitan District Commission (MDC), meant in 1970 when he said his agency had seen the light and realized "the immense potential" of the Hatch Memorial Shell on Boston's Esplanade. Why, until that definitive moment it was thought that 20,000 was a passel of folks to be cavorting on the banks of the Charles River. That, of course, was before it was somewhere determined that locals should visit this particular section of the Charles in roughly the same numbers that Hindus visit the Ganges.

And so it came to pass that the Hatch Shell became the location of some extraordinarily large gatherings during the mid-1970s. When 150,000 people showed up for the Fourth of July Pops concert in 1975, an MDC official termed the whole thing "unbelievable." He had not seen nothin' yet. On the subsequent two Fourths, an average of 350,000 people arrived for the music and fireworks. At a rock concert this past April, 175,000 wine-swilling kids bridged the gap between Hitler Youth and Woodstock. In other words, the three events combined to draw more souls to this small urban plot than currently reside in eleven of these United States.

Clearly the sky is the limit. I mean, if 3500 workers can daily fit themselves onto the one city block of the John Hancock Tower, how many people can line a river bank? One million? Two? The entire population of New England? A six-lane highway called Storrow Drive couldn't kill off the Esplanade, so how can it be destroyed by a few Porta-Potties? The only occasion when anyone worried about too many people being at the Hatch Shell came during World War II, when it was thought the Germans might attempt to bomb the place during a concert. But in the age of the neutron bomb, such precautions are a waste of time.

Think of all the years Boston has been trying to build a new sports stadium when it had one in its midst all the time. Listen, the Red Sox and Yankees draw only 35,000 people during the best of times, a mere handful by current Hatch standards. Were the Pinstripes and the Hose to square off regularly on the Esplanade, there's no telling what the American League attendance record might be. It is conceivable the Sox could reach what broadcasters like to call the "magic million mark" in a mere three-game series.

Parking? Nothing to it: simply blacktop the Charles. The engineering would be no more difficult than building a garage under Boston Common, the political corruption no more evident.

The Patriots could use the space during the fall, and the shell itself could be turned into a giant beer concession to insure the happiness of their well-lubricated fans. This would actually be in keeping with the structure's historic past, in that the first Boston Pops concert, held on July 4, 1929, featured beer-garden music.

With so much space to share, it's quite possible the Bruins and Celtics could play simultaneously. Perhaps they might even play each other, with the Pops entertaining at halftime. Instant replays of "The Ride of the Valkyries" could be shown on a giant TV screen above the shell itself, with slow-motion close-ups of the violins during crucial moments.

The mind boggles at the endless possibilities we've been passing up: Evel Knievel leaping the Charles, Muhammad Ali vs. your kid sister, Led Zeppelin arriving via dirigible for a concert. Now *that's* "immense potential."

Naturally there will be a few pessimists amidst all this progress. John Snedeker, the current MDC commissioner, was quoted in the aftermath of the April rock concert as saying, "I can assure you it won't happen again." But as any resident of Beacon Hill or Back Bay can attest, such wild promises have been made before. Rumor already has it that next year's Fourth of July celebration on the Charles will feature the firing of human cannonballs during the 1812 Overture.

The Garden Is Gone

THE KILLER is certain to arrive any day now. He has already done his dark deeds in neighboring places and is moving this way just as surely as the leaves turn and teal gather for their journey south.

There were times when I was so out of touch with the Maine countryside that I never paid any heed to the killer's comings and goings; for all I cared, he could fill the night with slaughter and cause me no grief. I was younger then, with less concern for johnny-jump-ups, zinnias, cosmos, mums and roses. I could walk right by rows of their corpses and never flicker an eyelash.

But now, now that I know the killer better, now that I can comprehend the vast scale of his crimes, now that I, personally, realize the nature of my loss, now that I know the awesome score I dread the coming of the killing frost.

I'm talking about that certain frost—the one that eliminates all wishful thinking that one tomato plant may have been spared, the one that verifies the end of all gardens, that puts a mark at the finish of the growing season more certain than any date on the calendar or phase of the moon.

You know what I mean. You can sense it in the stillness of the October evening, the chill clarity of the starry sky. It's a cruel beauty, this windless brilliance; it allows the killing frost to do his work without moderation from the clouds or disturbance by the wind. The way to the garden is quite without defenses and the cold moves in, flowing close to the ground on invisible rivers of malice. Newspapers spread about, tarps hastily pulled over the tomatoes, smudge pots lit, hay heaped here and there—none of it works against the merciless advance of a true killing frost. When you inspect the scene of the crime on the white, still morning after, there is a finality so evident that hope for survivors never even flickers.

The garden is gone.

If I put as much work into the garden as the true gardeners in the family do, I don't know how I could face this end. I am a taker from the garden, not a giver. The Master Gardener and her helpers (willing and not so willing) put in the seeds, the seedlings and the bulbs. But I get the benefits. They are there every day through the spring, summer and until the killing that's on its way. There are vases full of the flowers: daisies, roses, stock, phlox, lilies, lilacs, bluebells, morning glory, pansy and dozens more whose names I may never learn. But I know their beauty, and it gives the house a touch of grace more sparkling than any man-made decoration could ever be.

Do we value flowers more as we grow older? I've been musing on that, and I've decided we do. There is something so generous in their giving, so short-lived in their loveliness, so vital in their essential beauty that flowers become a kind of symbol of what is best about life; and, learning to love life better as we realize its approaching limits, we tend to keep more flowers around us as dual reminders of vitality and grace. There has got to be something there; otherwise why would I walk around with scissors, gathering new blossoms for the pitcher in my office, or the bowl in the center of the dinner table? I never did that in my thirties; I walked right by rows of frost-killed flowers without a twitch.

I don't anymore. What I do now that October is here is to be grateful that we live hard by the bay—such a vast, watery presence that it holds summer past September and is a warm fortress against the frost that has already browned gardens just a few miles inland. What I do is value each night that we escape the killer's coming; and what I do is gather the flowers and tomatoes each day in a kind of desperation, knowing as I do that the time for such pleasures is so short.

I know what I'm supposed to say: I'm supposed to look past the killing frost to next May's renewal. Perhaps I'll be able to do that in December. Now I can only shudder and await the killer that's certain to come.

135

A Few Kind Words for the Winter of '78

I KNOW, I know. Winter officially ended last week and you haven't been so happy to see anything leave town since former Red Sox manager Darrell Johnson outran the tar and feather mob. The season will go down in history as Don Kent's Revenge. It will be recalled as a fate worse than spending a weekend in Cleveland watching the Cuyahoga burn.

But wait. While this may seem a bit like saying Son of Sam was nice to his dog, I'd like to put in a good word for the winter of '78. God knows it could use a few friends. The critics have been carping, the nabobs nattering. The snow was the brunt of so many mindless jokes it could qualify as an honorary Pole. Television weather forecasters have been forced to wear bags over their heads in public.

Me, I think winter is getting a bum rap. True, my house was not whisked away to the coast of France at high tide. And I did not have to heat my home with cans of Sterno. For many people, the past few months have been little short of terrifying, and I do not mean to make light of their situations. But for the rest of us— particularly those in Boston during the storms—the winter was well worth the price of admission. I almost wish there had been a second show.

Look at it this way. In what other town could you have skiied to a National Basketball Assn. game? (Answer: Buffalo. Reason you wouldn't want to live there: Buffalo.) Sure, you could reside some place warm such as Los Angeles, where it seldom rains because the smog cover is watertight. Or you might try Florida, where Anita Bryant is among the least of the problems.

But that's my provincialism showing. The real reason winter was so delightful was that it taught us so much. If there hadn't been so much snow in February, for instance, who would have known that human beings will not eat okra under even the most dire circumstances? Yet the proof was right there in my neighborhood grocery store: an entire frozen food chest, empty except for sixty-three untouched packages of frozen okra.

There were other discoveries to be made. Bostonians learned what they had suspected all along, namely that their city does not need automobiles in order to survive. With the streets reclaimed by pedestrians during the storms, strange and wonderful sounds of silence filled the urban canyons. Perhaps a year in jail for anyone caught driving in the city should have been made a permanent, not a temporary, solution.

But the big surprise was the utter friendliness and charity displayed by city folk during periods of crisis. Under normal circumstances, a traveler asking assistance of a stranger in Boston might expect to have his ears bitten off for his trouble. In February, however, it was difficult to walk the streets without assorted do-gooders springing from doorways and trying to come to your rescue whether you wanted to be rescued or not.

And then there was the new vocabulary that was implanted in our brains as a result of winter. Reportorial language is frequently given to cliches, and by the time the season's second major storm had subsided we were buried under more verbiage than snow. I suppose this is to be expected when an awesome raging blizzard buffeted by hurricane-force winds makes streets impassable and turns snow-clogged arteries into a winter wonderland.

So lay off winter, will you? You'll miss it plenty in August when the temperature hits ninety-five degrees ("A real scorcher!") and the air conditioner breaks down and the car overheats on the way to the beach and there's a two-hour traffic jam at the Sagamore bridge and you've got a second degree sunburn. Just see if anybody tries to rescue you *then*.

Disorder Don't Come Easy

IT IS the easy order of the natural world which so often sets me to puzzling over the compulsive order we try to impose on it. I mean, trees grow their own complete way, making certain the seeds are planted for other trees to follow. And even when calamity strikes the forest—fire, drought, erosion—trees work over the centuries to restore the conditions that once were. The entire process takes place without apparent effort; it is the easy order of the natural world. It is only the presence of Man which mars the essential neatness of the woods. Without the beer can here, the flip-top there, or the crush-proof box by an abandoned campsite, the forest would be tidy, ordered, complete unto itself with every twig in place, every fallen leaf properly composting.

If we are all natural creatures (and I believe we are) then why can't we order our lives like the forest? Why, instead, must we spend days of each year trying to keep possessions in their proper place? Somewhere along the line, over the centuries as we became more "civilized," and less the children of nature, we imposed on ourselves the onerous burden of keeping order, and it is my observation that the burden grows more ponderous with every passing year.

Why is the matter so much on my mind? Because October has begun, and I know that before this month is past I must set the barn to rights. In the spring, when April quits her cruelness and gentles with May's approaching warmth, I am enthusiastic about the chore. The barn is cluttered with winter, and that season's disposal is a happy event. I can work cheerfully over a weekend in the musty barn, sweeping the scraps of a hundred sessions of kindling splitting, storing the snowshovels in the loft, searching for the dory oars, and taking inventory of the garden tools.

That April ritual is confirmation of better days to come, and I do not ponder for a moment the compulsions within me that insist

138

on setting the rakes in one place, the half-cans of paint in another, and the coils of rope each on their own peg on the barn's back wall. When the session is complete, I can stand for a full half-hour in the wide doorway, admiring the order of my work the way a painter regards a canvas he has completed to his full satisfaction.

Now that October is here, I walk quickly by the same doorway, knowing that if I pause to look I will see only the chaos of a summer gone. There is the fractured skeleton of a kite; it looked airborne even in repose in the store where we bought it, but once aloft it survived only moments before it hurtled to its own self-destruction. The ropes that had been coiled are sagging in sloppy piles with neither beginning nor end; paint brushes stiffen with permanent rigor mortis in abandoned cans; and in the corner a bag of lime purchased to sweeten the garden soil has been struck by a shovel blade and spills its insides in a pale cataract on the dark floor.

What a mess. How could it have evolved so quickly? The trees around me have been through the same summer, and they are scarcely rumpled. Their leaves are turning with the dignity of the equinox, their roots are taking firmer hold for the November winds to come. In the easy order of the natural world, the forest around me transits from summer to winter with the same certain grace that a river round a bend or a cliff rises at the edge of the sea. But you and I can not share that serenity. We must rummage in barns, cellars, closets and attics, doing our best to put the tattered tools of one season in their place, while we search the corners of our memory to locate the accessories we need for the winter on its way.

I have some friends up-country. They moved into a farmhouse that had been abandoned, and they live there in the glow of their creative work as artist and writer. In the Maine way, their barn is attached to the old house—a huge gray schooner of a barn sailing past the skiff of a house. I looked into that barn once. Centuries of seasons were there, piled one upon the other, gathering dust, scores of autumns, winters and springs, jumbled with the joys of summer—all there, complete in their total chaos, and brightened at their edges with the cast-offs of the new tenants, the easy-going folk who tossed their possessions on the pile without a thought of order.

That couple has mastered the easy order of the natural world. What I want to know, is when will I acquire the same sense of casual disorder. I already know it won't be this October. Whatever else I do, I'll set our barn to rights.

CITYSIDE / COPING

A Lament for that Plywood Status Symbol

IN THE spirit of not missing the water till the well runs dry, let us all turn our faces into the reflected urban sunlight and bemoan the loss of plywood. Plywood, you say? Yes, plywood, an acre of which once hung so inelegantly over the city and brought us the attentions of national magazines and network anchormen.

We should fess up. The John Hancock Tower, when it was sheathed in knotholes, was our secret pride and joy. Its sixty-story self was proof that you can kiss a princess and turn her into a frog. Here were the powers behind the largest financial institution in New England, using their muscle to have Boston's zoning laws amended so they could build a rhomboid-shaped status symbol. And what happened? Why, they couldn't get the darned thing to work right, that's what. How we shouted our I told you so's.

Those were certainly the days. Airline pilots banked their planes over the city in order to point out the wooden silo of Copley Square to their passengers. Tour buses devised new routes to show their gawking customers this strange sight. Visitors forsook the Freedom Trail so they might peer into the sky and see a chunk of glass plummet to the street. On windy days the Boston Police Department rushed in where pedestrians feared to tread and quickly roped off the area.

Bostonians who couldn't remember the name of their mayor could inform you that Hancock's 10,348 double-paned windows weighed 500 pounds apiece, cost $700 each and collectively covered sixteen acres. People who hadn't laughed in years walked around town telling woodpecker jokes. And almost everyone who heard the tale of Hancock's pane in the neck had a causal theory, usually involving corporate chicanery or the wrath of God or both.

I know about such conjecture because I was on the case. Having written a couple of stories about the tower's troubles, I soon became a clearinghouse for all sorts of speculation. There was the Cambridge woman, for example, who insisted that the windows were being shot out by a sniper who lived in a church steeple in her neighborhood. She was convinced the marksman was practicing on skyscrapers before he got down to the serious business of picking off human beings. I carefully explained to her that her theory was an unlikely one because large quantities of bullets had not been found inside the Hancock Building.

"Of course not," she replied without skipping a beat. "The building is made of glass, isn't it? The bullets go right through."

But of course.

There was also the man who sent detailed schematic drawings, complete with scientific formulae, which allegedly explained the windows' demise. The letters ran on for pages and inevitably came to the conclusion that the only plausible explanation for the damage was sabotage from within. He eventually became known as "Deep Note."

The principals, of course, did not share the public's sense of being entertained. As the news media like to put it, officials were "grim-faced." Mum formally became the word on Jan. 20, 1972, when high winds broke sixteen panes of glass up to the thirty-second floor of the building. This was fifteen days after a Hancock

141

executive had emphatically announced that the problem was confined to an area between the ninth and sixteenth floors. We the people reveled in his surprise.

But we have none of that now. True, Hancock occasionally assigns spotters to the streets beneath the tower. Their task is to keep a binoculared eye out for fractures. But the last such incident occurred eight months ago. It's just not easy for us to keep our interest up any more. Deep Note hasn't been heard from in months. And the lady in Cambridge recently called to say that the guy in the steeple must have run out of bullets.

Getting Around

Riding the MBTA Trail

THOMAS WOLFE once wrote that women are like streetcars, the theory being that if you miss one there'll be another one along in five minutes. Wolfe may have known something about females, but he obviously hadn't ridden the MBTA's Green Line in several years.

Take A. J. Deutsch. He knew. In 1950, he wrote an allegedly fictional account entitled "A Subway Named Mobius," about a Cambridge-bound train that disappears for weeks. Those of us who currently commute on the Red Line would certainly not deny the plausibility of such a tale. And what about the Kingston Trio? Do you really think it was an accident that Charley got trapped on the MTA and not on, say, the IRT?

Things like this are easy to write, of course, since the MBTA is about as popular hereabouts as gun control in Casper, Wyoming. However, as Lyndon Johnson once pointed out about the presidency, it's the only one we've got. Ken Campbell, who handles public relations for the MBTA, recently termed his position "a bit

145

discouraging in terms of rider complaints." Campbell has apparently learned his job well. I suspect that being a flack for the Green Line must be about as easy as writing press releases for Heinrich Himmler.

On the other hand, I admit to being something of an MBTA fan. (And an MTA fan before that, and—just barely—an El fan before that.) While it certainly doesn't maintain the gleam of Montreal's system nor the speed of London's tube, neither does the oldest subway in the United States feature armed guards. That is a piece of Americana best left to New York, and the people there are welcome to it.

The way I see it, the MBTA is being sold to all the wrong people—or at least that is the case with the 61.55 miles of routes we are continually requested to call the "Green," "Blue," "Red" and "Orange" lines. The wonderful thing about the 250,000 people who ride these lines on a typical weekday is that they are the best show you will find for a quarter. In fact, rather than sending tourists traipsing around the city chasing something someone has decided to label the "Freedom Trail," the Chamber of Commerce would do well to urge every visitor to make his or her way into the octopus of Park Street Station. *That* and all its tentacles, is Boston.

We are constantly being told that this is a city of neighborhoods. "Compartments" is probably a better word. As a result, you don't have to get off the MBTA to know precisely where you are. You don't even have to look out the windows. You can just sit there (or stand, if you happen to be on the Green Line) and let the city come down to you.

No veteran rider, for instance, is ever going to mistake the package-toting matrons who ride the air-conditioned cars into Quincy Square for the hunched desperadoes who travel the quaking Blue line to Wonderland. Hockey skates mean North Station, suitcases indicate Logan Airport, white socks announce Revere. Boston being what it is, a passenger traveling north on the Orange Line knows he has reached Washington street Station when all the blacks get off the train and all the whites get on. As for the infamous Green Line, it would remain a rare opportunity to view Boston's "youth culture" were it not for the fact that many kids long ago learned that it is far swifter to hitchhike.

Like the rest of Boston, the MBTA was built as a patchwork of seemingly unrelated pieces. It is as if the shaky hand of God kept re-cutting a giant jigsaw puzzle. According to one newspaper account of 1897, the first trolley into the Boston subway "hissed along like a brood of vipers." That is a better review than was received by the Riverside branch when it opened in 1959, and it is more than can be said for a modern Arborway trolley that sits beneath Copley Square for half an hour during a steamy August rush hour.

Consider. Where will you find a symbol of bureaucratic indifference to rival the change-maker who looks at a five dollar bill as a rude intrusion on his daily reading? What else can cause mayhem as amusing as the wino who ricochets from passenger to passenger high above Washington street in the South End? And where else will you see—as I recently did—a giddy customer tacking up a scribbled but mimeographed poster inviting everyone on the train to a party:

"Let's do it again!
Sat., 29, 1975
114 Norwell Street
Plenty of everything.
See you there!"

Rather than pay $2 to see a film entitled "Here's Boston," which is now showing in the Prudential Center, tourists should be hustling across Boylston street to the subway sign marked "Auditorium." A couple of hours on the MBTA will show them more urban elegance and squalor than they will ever get inside a theater. Where are you Thomas Wolfe, now that we need you? Rewrite that simile. Try this: "The MBTA is like a dangling love affair. You hate the bitch, but you keep going back."

Back Road Rider

THERE ARE several roads from my hometown and work-town to the Maine state capital where the lawmakers are now riding toward the crest of the current legislative session. On days when the weather is fair and I have a comfortable helping of time for the trip, I take the country roads to Augusta. Years ago, I used to live in one of the small towns between here and there, so I know nearly every one of the less traveled byways.

I like making the trip because these roads wind through some of the most authentically rural places in all of Maine, and perhaps New England. The relatively fertile lands in the lower valley of the Kennebec River still can support farming, and if the soil is not plowed for corn or carrots or parsnips, it is cultivated for hay and supports quite a few operating dairy farms. The open land is patched with wood lots—stands of hardwood and pine that also make a contribution to the rural economy.

Few of the gritty and determined folk who work their land make enough from one sort of farming to survive; instead, they are skilled at a number of pursuits and labor at them year-round. They fish the Kennebec for what few species have outlasted the river's intense pollution, they may grow a few Christmas trees, they tap their maples for syrup, and, at this time of year, they harvest some of the timber on those woodlots.

If the land has been in the family for a spell—say five or six generations—the harvesting is gentle. These Yankees learned long before Earth Day about the renewable resources that are pine, spruce, oak, maple, hemlock and birch. Because these wood cutters are conscious that their fathers, grandfathers and great-grandfathers were helped through the deep winter by the wood-lot's blessings, and because they are aware that their sons and daughters will also need to be helped in the future, they cut with care.

The trees that come down are mature; they are felled with an eye toward a clean fall—one that does not strip limbs from younger trees. The work is done quickly, energetically, but well. When the frost is deep, the forest floor will suffer least as the logs are skidded out. And, if there is snow on the ground then several of the woodcutters are able to use the teams of oxen and horses that still work in these woods.

That's why I take the back roads in February when a bright sun shines on the snow; I look for the teams. I find the sight vastly reassuring. The oxen puff great white snorts of steam as they pull; the flanks of the horses smoke in the sun. Even though there may be sentiment, the wood cutters here will deny it and defend their teams with arguments about how much less expensive they are than a $30,000 mechanical skidder, how much less harm they do to the fragile undergrowth, and how much more rewarding it is to achieve harmony with two oxen than with a snorting machine and its hydraulic controls.

I agree, and see the teams as something more. For me, the oxen and the horses—the "creatures" as the countrymen call them—are a symbol of the family land, the "place" that produces crops, grows hay, nourishes a woodlot, and allows those who care for it with work and concern to live lives that are quite in harmony with nature, relatively free of the compulsive need for more and more money. Yes, these rural custodians of the land need money, but they do not need as much as most and what they do need they can earn by becoming partners with their land.

It is a partnership of such sensitivity and complexity that it must evolve over generations; it is most difficult, for example, for outlanders, however dedicated and determined, to establish the relationship. (How many folks do you know who can steer two tons of oxen with a whisper and a pat of the hand?)

I see these stewards of the land as an important presence, one from which each of us can learn, one which should be maintained, one which is somehow crucial to the strength of this nation. But in the capital of Maine, and its counterparts in every rural state, the lawmakers seem unable to dismantle those parts of the property tax that are forcing the keepers of generational farm land off their places.

I wish the legislators could ride with me on the back roads when the teams are working in the sun.

The Guerilla Urban Traffic System (GUTS)

ACTUALLY, I don't know why I even bother to own a car. I keep toying with the notion of abandoning it in the dead of night, perhaps beneath the surface of the Charles River. The only thing that stops me is the suspicion that it would probably float, since its components are undoubtedly lighter than the muck which makes up the Charles. Besides, I know that even if it did sink, the meter maids would find it, and it would not surprise me if there is a $15 fine for parking under water.

So I continue to hang onto my 75,000-mile tribute to Japanese ingenuity, parking it on the city's streets by night in the hope it will somehow be gone by morning. No such luck, what with car thieves having better domestic and foreign targets than my well-dented survivor of urban living. As much as possible, I leave its operation to the woman with whom I live. (I once tried to have its title transferred from my name to hers, a seemingly simple undertaking in light of the fact we share the same last name. But no. The Registry of Motor Vehicles, or the computer which runs it, wasn't up to the task.) Yet there are days when I must ultimately face Boston traffic myself, and while these are the times that often lead me to my auto/aqua fantasy, I must also boast that I am a master of the Guerrilla Urban Traffic System (GUTS).

To be truthful, I must report that GUTS was taught to me by a cabbie known as ITOA Izzy. It had been passed on to him by another taxie driver, but as Izzy pointed out, almost anyone who lives in Boston for a month or two learns to drive with a variation of GUTS. Basic to the concept of the system, he explained, is the theory that the driver and the pedestrian are always in an undeclared state of war. In fact, Izzy often marveled at the fact that the local pedestrian population is seemingly unaware of what happens when 150 pounds of warm body comes into sudden contact with 4000 pounds of cold steel. "See them!" Izzy would shriek through the Plexiglas as we bore down on a group of unconcerned jaywalkers. "If God wanted them in the streets, He wouldn't have built sidewalks!"

So the first rule of GUTS is to treat the presence of pedestrians in Boston with approximately the same warmth and respect the Arabs show toward the presence of Israelis in the Middle East. Which is easy enough, since you know the feeling will always be returned. But there are other axioms. One states that the white lines on streets have been painted there only as a means of keeping city DPW employees from going home early, and for no other reason. They are therefore to be ignored, except perhaps as islands for meandering foot travelers.

Driving with GUTS in Boston also means that left-hand turns must be made from right lanes, and vice versa. Naturally, this is not easy when the previous rule has eliminated the recognition of lanes in the first place. Izzy likes to make his turn in a sort of wide arc, swinging, for instance, to the right and then swerving abruptly to the left. He feels this is his own contribution to GUTS and is proud of its ability to cut off other drivers both coming and going.

With GUTS, of course, traffic lights develop their own special meanings. Yellow is the signal to speed up. Red means slow down and look before crossing an intersection. Blinking lights indicate potential skirmishes with pedestrians. For some reason, GUTS doesn't mention solid green.

151

GUTS is to be used at any and all times in Boston, with one exception. This occurs when you are searching for a parking space either downtown, in Back Bay, or on Beacon Hill. An uninitiated visitor might think that all rules are suspended at such moments, but nothing could be further from the truth. As ITOA Izzy knows, the sight of a place to park means an automatic switch to the regulations of Chasing Hurriedly After Overt Space (CHAOS). And let me tell you, the fenders of my car are nothing short of homage to CHAOS in Boston.

COUNTRYSIDE / GETTING AROUND

Snow on the Sea

MY ONETIME friend and neighbor, Charles Preble, who lived most of his good eighty-four years in Maine, told me snow had been recorded in each of the twelve calendar months during one cold, Maine year that had etched itself deep in his memory. I believe him, but for me November is the month of snow, the mark on the year's index that assures me the ground will be white before the next thirty days are gone.

I don't let the thought trouble me the way it once did. Snow is part of Maine, as much as clambakes, cord wood and mayflowers; it arrives in its season and if it piles so deeply in the drive that the plow takes several days to reach us, so be it—I delight in the relative isolation, the break in the routine.

Those who fish the north Atlantic for a living, however, see snow in a different way. Like shaved ice dropped in a glass of wine, snow quickly cools the sea, and does it most effectively in the relatively shallow, inshore waters where fish and fishermen alike both congregate during the more temperate months. All fish inhabit definite and precise thermal limits, and when their habitat cools by a degree or two, they leave for more stable environments.

Thus one robust November snowfall can set entire marine populations in motion, either ending their availability entirely or forcing fishermen to take their boats miles offshore to deeper, and more hazardous, waters.

There is, of course, nothing a fisherman can do about snow's inevitability, but I remember how hard I used to try. By the last days in October I could always tell just how widely my hopes for the fishing season were going to miss their mark. Those wishful dreams of hauls that would balance the family budget, pay the grocery bills and put some folding money in the Christmas cookie jar would be blown away by the cold chills of late October. In their place would come a kind of desperation, a clutch at the hope for one last bonanza, one school of fish so large and so misguided that somehow our crew would find it, net it and sell it at the higher market prices that late autumn always brings.

As long as the snow stayed away, I could hang on to that hope. I could tell myself and my bill collectors that there was yet the chance to recoup an entire season with just a bit of luck. But the snow always came. It blew into my face, riding the shoulders of the northerly winds, sliding into the gray-green sea as silently as it melted on my cheeks where it sometimes mixed with my tears of frustration. The same flakes that covered the dory's scars also buried my dreams.

Porpoises put their mark on the first snow of one of my fishing Novembers, and it is the one I have seen every November since. The afternoon skies were dark with gray clouds that rolled like cannonballs from horizon to horizon, a northwest wind had flattened the swells and we were there on the beach, looking for fish and huddling in the hissing sand. As we crouched in the dory's lee, I could see fat flakes of snow slanting into the surf, white against the green sea.

But even as pain of lost hopes grew inside me, a school of striped bass showed on the outer bar and appeared to be moving inshore. We jumped up, yelling, backed the dory down, ready to set the haul seine. My dreams revived, even as the snow fell

153

harder. Then, just beyond the bass, a school of large porpoise surfaced; it was their predatory presence that had chased the bass into the shallows. We dared not set, knowing the net would be shredded by the scores of porpoise that moved into the breaking waves in their chase.

We stood there watching as porpoise exploded from the surf. I can still see one, high in the air against that leaden sky. Black as ebony except for a startling white bib, the porpoise had a bass in its jaws and the fish's blood streaked crimson on the white porpoise throat. The creatures fell back in the sea in a welter of ivory foam and, in a few minutes, both porpoise and bass had gone, leaving us, fishless until the spring, standing silent in the season's first snow.

For me, those porpoise still leap each November.

CITYSIDE / GETTING AROUND

At Home on Four Wheels

A MONTH OR SO ago, there was a great hue and cry in my neighborhood: much gnashing of teeth, pulling of hair, and shaking of fists in the direction of City Hall. It seems that Boston's Traffic and Parking Commission, a body whose wisdom frequently escapes many persons who live in the city, had decreed that residents must now park their cars exclusively on the odd-numbered sides of the street between midnight and 8 A.M. The alternative to this bit of apparent delirium was announced as a $15 fine. Some of you living in the great beyond (meaning Brookline and points yonder), may be mystified that such a pronouncement could cause outrage, but that is because you have never spent an entire evening circling the block. It is a well-known fact that most abandoned cars in Boston have simply been abdicated by drivers who have been unable to find a bit of earth on which to park. Thus, it is not surprising that when the commission sent down an edict that wiped out a sizable chunk of what little turf there is, a few of my neighbors were heard to be planning a sit-in at the Needham home of its commissioner, William T. Noonan. They thought they might hold it in his driveway.

Alas, what these outraged urbanites do not perceive is that Noonan and his cohorts are only trying to do us a favor. What the commission is attempting to accomplish is twofold: eliminate the housing shortage and save us money. Their plan is a bold one. Basically, they are determined to get Bostonians to live in their constantly moving automobiles. As ludicrous as this may at first appear, financial facts alone reveal its brilliance. For example, a car moving at ten mph and getting fifteen miles to the sixty-cent gallon of gasoline will burn $9.60 worth of gasoline in a twenty-four hour day, or $288 a month. Now $288 may be a steep rent in many sections of Boston, but it is certainly not unheard of in a city where $300 studio apartments are regularly advertised. Besides, if you are employed in a community which happens to allow parking, you can save approximately $67 a month on gasoline during working hours. And don't forget that your housing on wheels is heated. Further money can be saved if routes are chosen with an eye toward stop signs and traffic lights. The benefit of not having to pay Boston's real estate tax goes without saying.

The commission's daring in taking such a step will undoubtedly be rewarded when the currently hostile citizenry finally perceives its benefits. Entire families will be brought together in harmony reminiscent of, say, taking a four-hour drive to the beach on an August Sunday with four kids and a dog in the back seat. Certain bodily functions may become a bit of a problem, but itineraries can be selected which include passes at various hotel lobbies. (The Sheraton Boston is particularly good, but the stare of the doorman at the Ritz-Carlton may be a bit intimidating.) Friends who are not lucky enough to own an automobile could be enlisted to turn up at certain predetermined points, where they would pass food and other necessities through the windows in the best tradi-

155

tion of Charlie-on-the-MTA. The Neponset Drive-In stands ready to provide entertainment if for some reason driving the streets of Boston is not entertaining enough.

There is, of course, the danger that maybe, just maybe, a driver of one of these four-wheeled gypsies will discover a parking space. The perils inherent in this are evident: fines, towing, vandalism, and the like. No one is more aware of this than the Traffic and Parking Commission itself, which has reportedly been working long and hard to come up with a way to eliminate parking altogether within city limits. It has been suggested in some quarters that Boston purchase several thousand automobiles to fill up all existing spaces. The commission is characteristically tight-lipped about its plans, but given its sensitivity to the problems of residents in the past, we can expect nothing but good news. With friends like this, who needs parking spaces?

COUNTRYSIDE / GETTING AROUND

Travels and Travelers

SCHOOL IS out, or will be sometime during the coming week, for the thousands of children in Maine's public school system. For college students and those at private schools, the summer began earlier. For each of all of them, for their parents, relatives and friends, the arrival of this week in June is the signal for the annual summer migration that puts most of the millions on the road, in the sky, on board ship or merely on foot on a quiet path through the woods.

It is the time for travel—a time whose impact is apparently impervious to shortages, wars, inflations, recessions and the almost certain knowledge that poison ivy awaits. Here in Maine, the state braces for this summer's estimated (and rather ruefully anticipated) ten million visitors. That number has climbed steadily

156

each year since the start of the sixties; statisticians and social researchers tell us the rate of growth will begin to level off within four years or so when the total tops thirteen million and the travelers begin to bump into each other more frequently than they are able to make contact with whatever may be left of Maine.

Personally, I disagree with the data sweepers. The urge to travel, especially to such adventurous coasts as Maine's, has always been compulsive. Most folk, regardless of age and wherewithal, simply can not resist the migratory notion, anymore than a wild goose can quell the push that sends it north in the spring and south in the autumn. We are each prisoners of a compulsion that has its roots in eons of human migrations that began with time's beginnings and continued until we fooled ourselves into thinking that air conditioning and furnaces could make seasonal movement unnecessary. Perhaps they can, but their presence is not relevant to the awakening of the urge to travel that blossoms with every June.

Beyond that primal push, the eternal search for self also fuels the journeys of many of the young, and it is that combination which puts so many of them on the road. Those among us, like myself, whose schools closed decades ago, are less likely to go a roaming. Indeed, any of us already ensconced on the Maine coast would be utter fools to leave it to look for other, better places to enjoy a summer. There aren't any.

But often, it is not places that are sought. The graduates of '76 and their off-campus contemporaries search more for adventure than for climate, more for excitement than for scenery. We have all done it. Several tens of summers ago, I left the cool green of the Atlantic and spent my days in the dry green of the fine forests of inland Oregon. When I returned from that incredibly parched season and smelled the sweet salt of the open ocean beach, I wondered aloud why I had ever deserted my home ground. Yet, even as I wondered, I knew there were more travels to be taken.

During that decade I roamed through more than a dozen states, across oceans and on into lands where languages and customs were so different I knew what it was to be a stranger in a strange land. Those times have come back to me frequently during past Junes when I was nudged (not hard enough to make a difference) by the primal push, and when they did, I'd tell myself that I had seen many places and that there was no need to travel more.

This June I am discovering that the argument has less impact than ever before. Not since I was released by the school's-out bell have I had such a difficult time with my migratory stirrings. It is because I have had to travel more frequently of late to do my job as a journalist, and on those trips I arrived at an understanding that has eluded me for many years. Because I was so engrossed in the search for myself when I traveled as a youth, I really never "saw" the many places that search carried me. Now that my identity is secure (for better or worse) I am seeing more of the places I visit, even if I have visited them before.

I'm quite certain this minimal insight has revealed itself sooner to almost everyone but me—which accounts for the popularity of travel that I could never understand. I mean, if I was preoccupied with myself in Oregon, then I assumed other travelers were gripped by similar concerns. Living with that assumption, I failed to understand the glamour of a transcontinental trip. Now I can understand: once the self is ordered (more or less) travel becomes infinitely more rewarding.

Now that school is out, perhaps we'll meet on the road.

CITYSIDE / GETTING AROUND

If the Cars Don't Get You, the Potholes Will

IT WAS five years ago last week that the City of Boston officially opened its infamous "Green Belt Bikeway," billing it with a straight face as "an easy one-hour ride from Boston Common to

158

Franklin Park." The seven-mile trip was so "easy" that the first riders required a police escort to ward off the threat of being maimed by automobile traffic. Today the Bikeway lies mercifully abandoned, its demise the result of the realization that bicycles and the Jamaicaway do not mix.

But the street fight goes on. Those of us who venture onto the city's highways and byways on our ten-speeds are appreciating a thrill experienced only by ourselves and perhaps a few kamikaze pilots and rugby players. You have not lived until you have traveled at a speed of twenty miles per hour, perched rather nakedly atop a twenty-three-pound hunk of steel and rubber, and seen someone open the door of a two-ton automobile directly into your path. And if the cars don't get you, the potholes will. Or the trolley tracks, broken glass, or exhaust fumes. Not to mention the bicycle thieves, which every passing stranger is immediately and perhaps rightfully suspected of being.

According to Section 11B, Chapter 85, of the General Laws, the bicycle is every bit as much a vehicle in Massachusetts as is the automobile. (Except if it collides with a car, whereupon the bicyclist is regarded by law as a pedestrian. Small consolation.) When it comes to Boston traffic, however, this seems a bit like telling the Christians that they were on equal footing with the lions.

Let's face it: Bikes are the Hub's transportation outlaws. The only bikepath in the entire city—which runs along the Charles River from the locks to Boston University Bridge—is owned by the Metropolitan District Commission. The city's Parks and Recreation Department has nothing of the sort to offer, nor has the Boston Parking and Traffic Commission seen fit to paint any bikelanes on existing streets. The first covered bicycle parking facility, opened last month on Congress street, isn't the city's at all—it is operated by the Museum of Transportation.

One local cycling guide suggests that the only safe and sane time to ride in Boston is on Sunday mornings. Which is fine if you're out for a joyride, going to church, or wending your way home from a rather long Saturday night. But if your bike is your way to get around, if it is your *transportation* (remember what the Wright Brothers did before they invented the airplane?), you must be blessed with all the imagination, determination, and instinct for survival of a cab driver. And usually that is not enough.

You can always recognize an inexperienced city bike rider. He or she wears toe clips, those fancy-looking devices which loosely strap your feet to the pedals. But not loosely enough if you have to stop suddenly, whereupon you ignominiously topple sideways onto the pavement. Such people also make the mistake of trying to bike somewhere in Boston on a Monday or a Friday afternoon at rush hour. This is merely foolish on a Monday, when automobile drivers are exceedingly hostile; it is downright foolhardy on Friday, when they are hell-bent on reaching home before the martinis run dry.

But the smart city rider knows the tricks. He spray paints his frame fuchsia to give his bike the slummy look so necessary to discourage thieves. He takes his front wheel with him when he parks. He never goes into the streets during rush or lunch hours. And he treats cars as anyone should treat anything that weighs twenty to thirty times as much as himself, particularly when he knows it might do anything at any moment for any reason.

Many non-cycling locals complain that bicyclists don't obey traffic rules, which is true. But consider their place in society. They are thought to be intruders on Boston's streets, even though they were there before the automobile. The municipal view seems to be to get rid of them in as large a number as possible. If that's not the case, what *was* the purpose of the Green Belt Bikeway?

160

Learn to Stay Home

AN OLD-TIMER remembered for me the other day what it was like before motorized snowplows, before automobiles, before getting back and forth to town every day, snow or no snow, became a kind of compulsion for country dwellers. By this season of the year in the days of horse-drawn transport, snow would be packed about two feet thick on the roads. Ever since early December, teams of oxen and horses had been hauling huge rollers over the roads after every snowfall. The large, heavy rollers served only to pack the snow, not remove it. There was no salt, no sand, no busted mailboxes—just byways of packed snow perfect for sledding or passable for a team pulling a sleigh.

When a lobsterman or a farmer needed to go to town to buy flour, salt, meat or other staples, he would have to hitch up his team, tend to the runners on the sleigh, and then hope the "road" would stay in good condition for the three hours or so it might take to get to the nearest store and back. With that sort of preparation, there were seldom any trips on which this or that was "forgotten," and if the sleigh driver left his glasses on the dry goods counter, they were liable to stay downtown for a month.

As I listened to the stories of the trips (and sometimes, if the bay were frozen hard enough, risky short cuts would be taken across the salt ice) I decided our family could do with a little more forethought and a lot less impulse travel. With all the offspring (more than a half-dozen, counting mergers, etc.) our driveway looks like a used (very used) car lot most of the time. Several college tuitions sit out there wrapped in fenders, bumpers and second-hand tires.

Each auto owner claims his or her vehicle is essential to their occupation, peace of mind, and the daily performance of their duties. I have long since given up arguing against that: I merely

161

make it absolutely certain that I will entertain no pleas for help with installment payments, gasoline money, or registration fees. But it bothers me, nevertheless, that all these vehicles seem to be in motion most of the time, and yet scarcely a day goes by when I don't get a call asking me to stop by on the way home for a pint of cream, a loaf of bread, a quart of milk, or a skate sharpener.

What I want to know is: why, if four other family vehicles have been out "cruising," haven't the younger, more energetic, less occupied folks in the family been able to get whatever the household needs, and more. Just what have they been doing out there on the asphalt all day—and sometimes all night. Even the Master Shopper herself has been known to spend most of the daylight hours in the shops and then, safely home, call on me to "pick up Sam's glasses," or "stop by the school, because he forgot his French homework."

What I cannot comprehend is: where did all these errands come from? Why, after just a relatively few decades (compared to centuries of civilization) with the internal combustion engine are so many otherwise practical rural folk apparently compelled to get behind the wheel every day of their lives: I think it is because we no longer truly understand "country living." Even though we have a snug home, even though—with a bit of planning—we have the facilities to hold a month's stock of supplies, we feel restless, housebound, and somehow out of kilter with the times if we don't hit the road once a day, at least.

If we had to stay at home for even two weeks, most of us would feel trapped somehow, although our "trap" might be one of the loveliest places in the world. So our taxes support a vast fleet of snowplows, our time payments go for snowblowers and automobiles so we can make our "escape" to nowhere whenever the fancy strikes us. There is always an errand that can be created.

What will happen, I wonder, when gasoline becomes so rare impulse trips are absolutely out? We will have to learn to live as our grandparents and great-grandparents did—taking a trip downtown on snow-packed roads only when it is positively necessary. We'll have to learn all over again to stay at home, content with and close to nature. As far as I'm concerned, we'll be the better for it.

Being Game about the Green Line

IT SEEMED like a bargain at the time. All I had to do was hand over $9.45 to the clerk in Filene's and she would present me with "The Boston Game." It came in an attractive multicolored box which promised in black type that I would learn HOW TO PLAY THE SUBWAY. (Provided, of course, my age fell somewhere between TEN and ADULT.) A steal at that price, I assured myself while collecting my change. I felt a rush of excitement as I carried my package homeward, a journey which was delayed only slightly by a fire in Park Street station.

I was not dissuaded when a flyer inside the box claimed that "Bostonians have long been fascinated by their transportation system," although making such a statement is a bit like claiming that Richard Nixon has long been fascinated by the press. The blurb went on to inform me that I was the proud owner of something which "lets you sit back and figure out how to beat the subway system for yourself." It exhorted me to "let those delays, repairs, and mix-ups obstruct your opponent's progress." It even promised to be an activity wherein "skill and chance work together," an appropriate pairing of the very factors which control the destinies of MBTA riders themselves.

Of course, I needed an opponent whom I could riddle with delays, repairs, and mix-ups. Since I am clearly ADULT, I chose Elias, who is TEN. He had recently reached the stage where he would no longer allow his mother to ride the MBTA without his assistance, so I knew he would be a worthy foe. He quickly learned

163

the rules and noted that the object of the game was to visit six of Boston's places of interest and be the first to return to the original starting point. "Normally that would take a week," Elias said, shuffling the deck of red "jeopardy cards" which would control our travels. "I have to be in bed by 9:30, you know."

As we moved our colored markers around the board—a replica of the MBTA's four alleged "Rapid Transit" lines—it was obvious that Elias was having difficulty coming to grips with The Boston Game's view of life beneath the streets of the city. Oh, he could identify with the rule which allowed us to close stations for repairs without apparent reason. And he understood the card which ordered him to SPEND THE DAY AT ASHMONT, since he and his mother had recently done precisely that after boarding a train which was clearly but erroneously marked QUINCY. It's just that the poor kid kept searching for things the game's inventor had somehow overlooked.

When I landed at Arlington, for instance, Elias didn't think I should be allowed to move again until at least a dozen trains had passed through the station traveling in the opposite direction. As I later moved my piece along the Red Line, he refused to let me make the jump from Andrew to Columbia without a ten-minute delay. When I arrived at North Station he again insisted that I stay put. "But why?" I asked, anxious to get to Haymarket where I could switch to the Orange Line for a fast run to Warren Tavern. "Because Aerosmith is playing at the Garden," he replied without looking up, "and their fans are trashing some trolley cars." Of course.

But it was evident Elias was also getting bored with The Boston Game. Something was still missing. Was it the wino who has sometimes serenaded him between Arlington and Copley? The guy who sings along with his cassette tape recorder on the Blue Line? The Park Street change-maker who becomes surly when faced with anything larger than a half-dollar? "Yeah," he answered, closing the board in mid-game. "I mean, where are the old ladies who'll break your leg to get a seat? Where are the loudspeaker warnings about the purse snatchers? Do you know," he added, lowering his voice, "that there's not even any graffiti in this game?"

The kid had a point. I mean, you can't really be educated in HOW TO PLAY THE SUBWAY in Boston without learning how to translate graffiti. Not even for $9.45.

COUNTRYSIDE / GETTING AROUND

On Footwear

IT IS about mid-February every winter that I grow weary of my feet. Not that I want to separate from them, you understand; I appreciate the need for ten toes, two soles and a pair of heels. It's what goes on over them that begins to test my mettle after two months of winter. It's a problem for many of us who live in the country, but feel constrained to affect some resemblance to our urban counterparts . . . like wearing shoes.

I watch for the way it was in the "old days" whenever I get a chance. Nineteenth Century photographs and/or paintings which depict everyday rural Yankees in winter are rather rare, but those that do turn up generally show the men of the times with their feet stuck in bulky furs. I could say boots, but the accoutrements of which I speak have little in common with what passes for boots today. As best I can tell from studying the pictures of the past, winter feet north of Boston were swaddled in mink and muskrat hides, and kept covered until spring.

Those of us living in the same places once toiled over by those big-footed forebears could hardly show up for work these days with our feet wrapped in mink. Just think of the commotion that would cause, even among the liberals. No, we must wear shoes if we want to be considered reasonably rational by most of our fellows.

165

But shoes don't work. I mean they don't work at the job they are ostensibly designed to do: they don't protect the feet, not against the conditions that face most of us here from December through March. You know what I mean—a foot of snow one day, a thaw the next, and then three inches of slush, a freeze the next, a thousand miles of glare ice, and a sub-freeze the next which drops thermometers far below zero, whether yours is Centigrade or Fahrenheit. Slush slips over the tops of low-cut shoes, or mushes in through the soles. Cold makes a mockery of rubber boots, congealing the toes after just a few outdoor minutes. Both sorts of foot coverings slip like otters on the ice.

One of Maine's more prominent and noble citizens, the late Leon Leonwood Bean, made a fortune and acquired proper fame by trying his best to cope with the problem. The Bean Boot is a combining of rubber, leather and insulation which attempts to conquer each of the changing weather conditions I have described. And it pretty well does, which is why about half the college students in the northern half of the nation wear Bean Boots (or imitations) through their winter semester.

Bankers, novelists, shop keepers, governors, editors, professors, engineers, and dermatologists, however, cannot emulate the student free spirit. More than decorum is required of us middle-aged professionals. It is our duty to reassure those who look to us for leadership by wearing shoes, at least to our places of business. Thus we search for boot substitutes. Some are still trying rubbers; you can see them every snowy day, lined up outside office doors. Others have rescued galoshes from their childhood; their arrivals and departures are punctured with grunts as the body is bent to haul the galosh on, or off.

Still others, like myself, try a compromise. There is a sort of boot-shoe that comes to ankle height, is lined with lamb's wool (or its synthetic cousin) and soled with rubber (or its synthetic cousin.) Like the Bean Boot, it does a decent job, especially if the leather (or its synthetic cousin) is rubbed well and often with mink oil— for which there is no synthetic cousin. This footgear looks almost like a shoe, but it does about three-quarters of what a full boot might do.

It's heavy, that's the trouble. After walking through an average fourteen-hour day (not all work, mind you) my legs feel as if they'd been burdened with a ball and chain. When I finally take off my boot-shoes, my feet tend to elevate, like a balloon set free. Which is why, along about this time of the year, I begin to get a bit weary of my feet. I know there's a spell to go yet, but I can't help starting to anticipate those glorious days just over the horizon— days when I can slip on a pair of sneakers, or loafers and walk across ground that is warm, dry, and full of the fragrance of spring.

CITYSIDE / GETTING AROUND

Taxiing toward a Fun City

CRITICIZING BOSTON'S taxicabs is about as controversial as taking a stand against earthquakes, ax murderers, or the Third Reich. It is the constant sport of politicians and journalists, partygoers and shoppers. The litany of sins is regularly recited: the cabs are dirty, unsafe, expensive, and unreliable. Alas, the list is more accurate than not. The Boston taxi often performs like a runaway armored car, bouncing over potholes with its locked fare box and bulletproof partition rattling loudly. It frequently gives the impression that something rather large and bulky is rolling around inside its trunk. (The previous riders' suitcase? A body? Pray God, a spare tire?) Air conditioning is all but nonexistent and Pepto-Bismol is required for digestive survival. The drivers themselves are generally friendly but often topographically confused. "We don't want rapists or sexual deviates driving cabs," an official of the City of Boston Cab Association was once quoted as declaring. However, most Bostonians would gladly travel to their destinations with a sexual deviate if only said driver could be counted on to know the way.

Yet such detractors miss the point. And so do all those people who get caught up in the city's annual "crackdowns" and "cleanups" of the local taxi industry. The fallacy in their reasoning lies within their basic premise, which states that the purpose of a Boston taxicab is to carry people from *here* to *there*. But that, of course, is not the principal function of such a vehicle. It's not for nothing that Governor Michael Dukakis would rather ride the Green Line to and from work.

What the Boston taxicab provides is an antidote to faceless, mechanized urban living. No two rides are the same. No two taxis take you from Point A to Point B via Route C. And even if they do, the fares are somehow different. To enter a taxi in the Hub is to embark on a magical mystery tour of assorted mechanical surprises and geographic wonders. It is common in some cities for cabbies to take unwary passengers for rides which are figurative as well as literal, meandering about town in order to increase their fares. This does not happen in Boston. Correction: the *meandering* happens, but it is not accompanied by scurrilous motives. You see, the only requirements for operating a cab here are a driver's license and a clean criminal record. Believing that the State House is located in Mattapan is not considered a roadblock to employment.

I am not a particularly heavy cab user. But I would guess that I make between 100 and 150 trips a year, annually leaving $500 behind in the hands of my chauffeurs. I consider the money well spent. Only last week a cabbie asked me from the front seat if I wanted to look at some postcards. My prurient interests aroused, I inquired as to their nature. The cards that he slid under the partition were pictures of the kind one finds in the desk drawer of one's hotel room in Las Vegas. Filthy stuff.

I once drove with a cab driver who had a coatimundi riding shotgun. The animal, a South American raccoon, seemed put off by the careening taxi. It kept nervously nibbling on the front seat.

Then there was the time my cab gave up the ghost in the Callahan Tunnel and I had to drag my suitcase along the catwalk, inhaling exhaust fumes for half a mile. I have encountered at least two cabbies who didn't speak English, and many more who didn't understand it.

But that's the fun of it, don't you see? In London, all the taxis look alike. In New York, all the drivers look alike. Boston is the taxicab badlands, the foaming frontier of rugged individualism where you jump aboard the stagecoach and hang on for the duration. Sitting in front of you is a hairy kid, a bald man, or a woman with an orange bouffant. What's the difference? Sit back and enjoy the ride to the airport. By the way, where is that?

COUNTRYSIDE / GETTING AROUND

Driving for Pleasure

FOR THOSE of us who like driving, there are gloomy days ahead. Oh, I know what the popular image of a rustic ought to be. Those of us who choose to live more than ten miles from the nearest restaurant and fifty miles from any building taller than a church steeple are seen by urban and suburban eyes as folks who like staying home, who won't venture on the public roads unless it's town meeting time, or the day has come when the monthly shopping must be done.

There are some country folk who do live by such schedules, and thank goodness for them. If they didn't, the rural roads around here would be more crowded than they are. And, as far as I'm concerned, conditions now are approaching the intolerable. I have long maintained that one of the supreme benefits of the countryside is the opportunity to utilize the road system the way it was designed to be used.

You know what driving in most of America is really like; it

seldom, if ever, bears any resemblance to the television versions which tease you into spending thousands for a new car by showing you young lovelies breezing along spectacular scenic byways with nary another auto in sight. If you come out of your TV trance, however, you realize that very little of your time behind the wheel is so carefree. Either you are locked into the monotony of a superhighway, or you are creeping from one stoplight to the next in rush-hour traffic.

Not so in the far reaches of the countryside, however, and especially not so in some of the more distant reaches of Maine—my country. If you like to drive—and by that, I mean if you truly enjoy a responsive vehicle that reacts when you shift gears and turn the steering wheel—then some of the best roads in the nation are here.

I realize my status with my environmental friends may never be the same again after this public confession. I mean, here I've been talking all these years about saving energy, doing more with less, appropriate technology, etc. etc. etc. Now I am revealed as suffering from a touch of motoring madness. Remember Toad (of Toad Hall fame) in *Wind in the Willows*? When he saw a new roadster go by he could not control himself; neither can I.

Not that I take to the roads on whim alone; I do not. I haven't the time for that. But if my work takes me here or there, as it often does, I choose the long way around, and always via the back roads. I find it peaceful and mildly exhilarating to motor along country lanes. I find the exterior landscape most tranquil, and, in the process of rounding curves and cresting hills, I have also discovered that my interior landscape is also enriched. I germinate and refine some of my most productive ideas as I drive between miles of Maine woods or past hayfields newly cut.

The only requirement is solitude. Put more than three vehicles in front of me, and I am transformed from constructive contemplation for the greater good of mankind to a self-destruct mechanism determined to take any risk to escape the Ford or Chevy that blocks my free passage. For me, all motoring magic vanishes with the intrusion of cruising couples, real estate hunters, lost moving trucks, camper trailers, and the barriers, flagmen and heavy equipment of road repair crews.

Thus I have arrived at a formula for my most fulfilling hours at the helm. I travel most on clear, cold days in January and February, ideally just a day or so after snow has fallen with some persistence. Rural plow crews have cleared the way; six feet of frost have ended any possible roadwork for construction crews, and the casual car pilots are in their reclining chairs, watching the auto ads on television.

I am out there motoring—free, alone, and quite unmolested. Those of you who have never been able to enjoy such freedoms know not what you are missing. But I warn you, it is too late for this year. As I have discovered during the recent weeks of warming, the construction people are back, the police patrols are vigilant, camper trailers have broken their silence, and all manner of casual voyagers are cluttering the asphalt. As I said, there are gloomy days ahead.

CITYSIDE / GETTING AROUND

In Search of Urban Heroes

AH, NEW YORK: always a step ahead. The fact that a young man named George Willig recently scaled one of the two 1350-foot towers of the World Trade Center was news enough. But what was really eye opening was the subsequent insistence by the natives that Willig be set free after his three and one-half hour caper. The city fathers, knowing a potentially ugly mob when they see one, hastily agreed. It is a wonder there was no ticker tape parade.

Actually, the authorities were undoubtedly relieved that their city's latest hero wasn't being revered for holding hostages in a bank or trying some other "Dog Day Afternoon" stunt. Nope, Willig is your classic American good guy who simply came, saw and conquered. God only knows how many newspaper reporters must have filed stories about venerable dame New York opening her heart to this example of youthful bravery. One could almost hear the brains of television commentators clicking into gear as they explained the reaction of the populace by lamenting the absence of urban frontiers to challenge.

As always happens in these cases, we are in for a rash of similar escapades. Like airplane hijackings during the 1960s, capturing a city's imagination by performing a feat of daring may become the accepted method of getting yourself on the six o'clock news during the late 1970s. And despite what you may have been told to the contrary, there are still plenty of Willigesque exploits to be considered in any town. Why, the next few years in Boston are bound to reveal a string of resourceful crazies. Consider the following possibilities:

• As a festive lunchtime gathering watches from below, Icarus Cosmopoulos of Hyde Park turns himself into a human kite by leaping off the top of the Prudential Building using wings constructed of pigeon feathers. Cosmopoulos is sailing along smoothly until he flies too low over the city incinerator, thereby causing the adhesive on his wings to melt and himself to plummet into Dorchester Bay.

• Efil K. Nefil, a Saudi Arabian immigrant, attempts to jump the Charles River on a moped. Working secretly during an entire night, the fearless Nefil constructs a launch pad on the Esplanade. Unluckily, the leap is somewhat less than successful when the Saudi fails to clear the Hatch Shell on take-off. Howard Cosell covers for ABC.

•A.J. Voight of Jamaica Plain sets the world land speed record by driving from downtown Boston to Logan International Airport in eighteen seconds flat. Eschewing the jet automobile typically used in such attempts, Voight instead drives only a standard ITOA taxi cab. Without shock absorbers, naturally.

• Lou Dini, an itinerant magician from East Boston, binds himself in chains, locks himself in a steamer trunk and rolls himself into the Fort Point Channel. After thirty-six hours without a word from her husband, Theresa Dini shouts into the water that she won't hold supper another minute for him. Dini immediately surfaces and is greeted by a cheering crowd.

• Mabel Flurg of Brighton enters a Green Line MBTA car one morning and vows to remain seated in it until her effort is recorded in the Guinness Book of World Records as the longest distance traveled by subway. After eleven days, Mrs. Flurg is still in the car. Unfortunately, it has traveled only three stops in that time.

Who knows? Tomorrow being the Fourth of July, maybe we'll see a human rocket flying over Boston. Perhaps an oldtime flagpole sitter will emerge. Or maybe George Willig himself will turn up, dressed in an Uncle Sam suit and climbing the east slope of the John Hancock Tower. Even cities which aren't New York need heroes.

COUNTRYSIDE / GETTING AROUND

"The Last Time I Saw Boston"

ABOUT THIS time—as I'm certain many of you either recall or have been recently reminded—a year ago, snow immobilized Boston. Almost as much printer's ink has been spread over that storm as there was snow itself. My concern has to do with my interior landscape, not the exterior evidence of meteorologic phenomena. That storm has a personal significance which I have pondered ever since.

Such events do not often stay on my mind for a year or more. I can, and do, relive the hurricane of '38 every now and then; that one nearly demolished our home on Long Island and if my mother hadn't been rescued from a second-floor window by Coast Guardsmen in a surf boat they navigated from the Georgica Life Guard Station, she might not have survived. I shared another hurricane, one September in the early Fifties, with Peter Matthiessen aboard his boat, the *Merlin,* at Montauk. Each of us, I think, remembers times of high adventure.

However, no personal risk attached to my circumstantial entrapment in Boston last February. The word "adventurous" hardly applies to my environment during the week of the storm. Yes, the electricity which powers the solid, comfortable (some might add elegant) Commonwealth Ave. apartment I inhabited failed for some six or eight hours, but the thick walls of the old "they-don't-build-them-like-that-anymore" building held enough heat within so my discomfort was negligible. I had only to walk two blocks to the Ritz—where service never faltered—to avail myself of the essentials for survival: food and drink, and with commerce quite disorganized, I could, quite legitimately, fail to show up for what little work could be done.

On their surface, the conditions of my life during that week were little less than luxurious; while I fretted about the stability of the Ritz menu, millions of other New Englanders were legitimately concerned for their survival, or the survival of their homes along the coast.

Yet my inner misery intensified, day by day, long night by long night, until, toward the end of that second week in February, I began to think that if I could not escape the City of Boston and return to my home in Maine, a mental and spiritual calamity of frightening proportions would overtake me. I said as much in my frequent phone calls to the family 130 miles from Commonwealth Ave. The response seldom varied. Assured that my physical health and personal well being were being handsomely sustained, they told me to relax and enjoy.

Alas, I could not follow those instructions. Ordered not to leave Boston, under penalty of police action, no other thought sat on my mind more heavily than the realization I could not go where I pleased, when I pleased. In my view, I was being held under house arrest.

As it did for everyone, there came a time when I could go home again. I know I shall never forget the excitement, the release of that ride back to Maine. I could not contain my joy, and when I reached home and ran up the front walk, I felt like a prisoner who had escaped from Devil's Island after being condemned to spend the rest of his life in solitary.

The family, I'm sure, worried about my condition. For them, it had been just another storm. Why, they wondered, had the senior member of the household, the so-called authority figure, come so undone?

That's the question I myself have pondered for more than a year now. The answer has to do, I have come to believe, with the difference between country life and city life. Freedom—whether we recognize it or not—is more purely available to more people in rural environments than it is to anyone in the city. Conversely, discipline, repression, authoritarianism—whatever the opposites of freedom—are practiced most extensively in cities: places where they are needed to control large numbers of people living in small spaces.

I had become too used to my unrecognized rural freedom to ever return comfortably to live, full-time, in a city. Last February's storm taught me that lesson by so intensifying aspects of urban totalitarianism. I'm back in the country now, somewhat the wiser for my lesson. I doubt very much if the "Blizzard of '78" had the same effect on anyone else.

Parking until Death Do You Part

As THE evening was drawing to a close, the young woman standing next to the ficus was making her post-party transportation arrangements. "I'm not driving tonight," she said, reaching for the last remnants of the avocado spread. "You see, I found a marvelous parking space right outside my building and I can't bear to give it up."

We stopped in mid-dip. Come again?

"I happened onto it three days ago," she explained. "On Wednesday. It had belonged to a red Fiat for several weeks when the owner abandoned it with no explanation. Luckily, I was driving past at the time. A turquoise Monza made a dash for it, but I got there first."

Let us see if we understand this, we said. Three days ago you found a parking space for your car outside your apartment building, and now you won't use the car because you'll lose the space?

"Of course," she answered. "This is Boston, dear boy. If you get a parking space you hang onto it until death do you part. If you're smart, you put it in your will. Why, the Bartleys over there postponed an entire summer in the south of France when they located a spot on Commonwealth Avenue."

We stopped a passing waiter, relieved him of two martinis, and raised the glasses towards the Bartleys in celebration of their good fortune.

"Naturally," the woman continued, "the city fathers make life rather difficult. What with street cleaning and all, the parking tickets are a bit much. Still, it's cheaper than driving, don't you think?"

We don't know what to think, we replied. We admit we are confused. What we take you to be saying is this: You own a car for the purpose of transportation but won't use it for said purpose because . . .

176

"Because I can't take it out," she replied, completing the sentence for us. "I mean, what would I do with it when I'm through with it? I just can't drive around and around looking a place to park. I have other obligations. I have a job. I have a family. Why, even the Bartleys can't afford to spend all their time behind the wheel."

We all looked toward the Bartleys, who were saying their au revoirs before departing.

"Oh, it's such a blessing not to have to think about it tonight," the woman was saying. "You can't know how miserable I used to be at parties like this, how much I was afraid of going home."

You have nothing to fear but fear itself, we pointed out. But tell us something. If you can't drive the car, why do you shell out God only knows how much money on payments, insurance and taxes? What we mean is, why don't you just get rid of the thing?

The woman looked stunned. She blinked from behind the tortilla chip which she had just crunched. "Dear boy, you haven't lived in Boston very long, have you?" she asked. "I mean, for one thing it's obvious you've never tried to take the MBTA. The MBTA, you will undoubtedly learn to your horror, does *not* run to Vermont on weekends. It stops a good half mile from Bloomingdale's in Chestnut Hill. And, as far as I know, it operates no line which surfaces in the vicinity of Nantucket Sound.

"You simply have to have a car here," she went on. "How would you shop without one? Or tailgate at the Yale game? Or . . ."

She was still talking when we slipped away, keeping the ficus between us and her. We made our exit quickly, striking up a brisk pace right behind the Bartleys.

You Can't Get Here from There

BY THIS time I can begin to believe it's over. The summer, I mean. Yes, there are the glories of a Maine September all around us; this is, I will argue, our finest season. Summer is also a climatic delight, especially here in Maine, but by this time each year I let myself wallow in the relief of knowing that it's gone. The traffic on Maine Street no longer chokes so that my daily trip takes thirty minutes instead of fifteen; the parking space in front of Day's News & Variety is not taken every morning when I stop for my daily newspapers; I do not wince now whenever the phone rings, hoping against hope that it won't be one more college roommate (how many did I have?), one more traveler who just wants to "visit for a minute" and stays the night with children and Russian wolfhound.

And, most of all, there is the restoration of domestic tranquility that comes when myself and The Lady no longer debate over who is going to give what directions to whom. I have no data on the topic, but I would wager a week's pay there can not be more than a dozen couples in all New England who agree that each of the two knows how to give directions. I would argue and wager, on the other hand, that every husband thinks every wife has no orientation whatsoever, does not know where she lives and can only succeed in getting touring visitors hopelessly lost whenever she attempts her endless narrative of "turn left at the cute little mailbox and then right—well, sort of right—at the lovely stand of rosa rugosa. . . ."

But for every husband who despairs enough to wrench the phone from the graceful hand of his otherwise exemplary helpmeet, there are the wives who will laugh out loud whenever the man of the house begins his "how you find us" spiel. "Go just four-tenths of a mile a bit east of south until you come to a large pine tree—and watch for the utility pole—and then west for another eight-tenths of a mile along the Point road until it forks to the north. . . ."

Both sorts of monologue (and the listener is usually trying to take notes with a hard pencil on a wet pizza plate) go on for most of a half-hour. When the visitor finally rolls into the yard, exhausted from a day on the hot highway and superlatively irritated by having had to stop fourteen times to ask suspicious strangers for directions, the direction giver always inquires, "Did you have any trouble finding us?"

The answer, coming from a known freeloader who can see a cool drink and an evening meal vanishing if there is further discord, always replies, "No, none at all. The directions were just perfect." Then, whosoever bestowed the instructions turns to hapless spouse and says, "See," through properly curled lip and with impeccable disdain. Thus the stage is set for yet another competition when yet another roommate (how many did I have?) calls and says he's on his way back from Nova Scotia and would love to drop by.

There was a time when I thought such directional discord was rampant only at our house, but having recently expanded my own swath as a traveling freeloader, I can report it is quite universal. So much so that I have made some attempt to analyze its causes in the interests of social history. It is not only the normal, and healthy competition between couples which prompts the "direction syndrome" but also the little noted fact that each of us sees our own home roads in quite different ways.

As individuals, we find ourselves looking hard at one tree, noting one garden, spotting one bird's nest, while our counterpart keeps track of the condition of one lawn, or the paint on another garage. Thus, when either tries to give directions, the other assumes he/she has taken leave of his/her senses.

I'm happy the summer and the arguments are over. Things got so bad I drew a map, had it copied and mailed out at least half-a-dozen. The knowledge that they are out there, in circulation, has me terrified about next summer and remorseful that I didn't let The Lady's directions suffice for everyone. That way, none of the callers could ever have found the house.

Riding on Hot Air

LAST MONTH, Boston Mayor Kevin White announced that he had scrapped plans for the city to purchase a $24,000 Lincoln Continental to squire visiting dignitaries around town. With the City Council baying at the proposal in its normal jackal-like manner, His Honor allowed as how famous tourists would have to make do with a 1975 Ford station wagon known principally for its loose tailpipe. "Let them eat fumes," the mayor seemed to be saying.

Now, however, tongues at City Hall are wagging about an as-yet unannounced scheme to purchase—are you ready?—a hot air balloon to ferry official visitors throughout the Hub. There's even a hot rumor (if you'll pardon the expression) that the mayor's image makers have already selected a catchy name for the craft: "Old Nylonsides."

Our source in this matter revealed a few other details during a recent interview inside the Boston Common Parking Garage. "The mayor figures the members of the City Council can't give him no grief on this one," our contact said, speaking deeply from the throat. "After all, they're already experts on hot air. Heh-heh."

"Seriously," the source continued, noting our stern demeanor, "what's the poor guy gonna do? I mean, the mayor of Akron comes to town for a visit, you wanna send him on an Arborway car?"

But isn't a hot air balloon a little risky, we wondered.

"You think maybe a '75 Ford is built by Ralph Nader?" he replied. "That's what you think? Listen, my friend, I'll tell you what 'risky' is. 'Risky' is 6:30 at night on the Southeast Expressway with the three-martinis-after-work crowd. Me, I'd rather be 100 feet up in the air any time."

Fine, we said. But won't this be a bit pricey?

"Nah," came the reply from the darkness. "The cost beats a Ford wagon any day. I mean, what's a little liquid propane gas? Besides, once the jets are turned off, it's all free as a bird—in more ways than one, if you get my drift."

But where will you park it?

"No problem. City Hall Plaza is just sitting there doing nothing. A perfect landing strip, you ask me."

We had to admit the plan was beginning to sound attractive. And we noted that a balloon would certainly comply with the City Council's recent ordinance forbidding the purchase of any car that gets fewer than twenty-two miles per gallon.

"You catch on quick," the source said. "Also, there's no pollution and no noise. I'd like to see those goons in the Council complain on this one, my friend, I really would."

Of course, we countered, New England weather is a little unpredictable. And balloons do drift with the wind . . .

"Hey lookit," our friend interrupted. "You can't have everything. So maybe the Mayor of Akron gets to see Thompson's Island instead of Back Bay. It's a nice trip anyway. And you sure couldn't get there in a Ford or a Lincoln, could you?"

No, you couldn't, we answered. But one thing was troubling us. Are there any licensed balloon pilots at City Hall to fly Old Nylonsides?

"Don't worry," the source replied. "We'll just have another driver assigned to the Mayor by police headquarters. Except in the summer, of course. That's when he'll have to find a nephew or someone like that for the job."

Autumn Voyages

THERE ARE voyages on my mind at this time of the year. That may seem an odd preoccupation for mid-autumn; for many it is a season of gathering, of storing, stocking, closing in, battening down, of earlier homecomings in the earlier evenings when families collect at the fireside feeling the warmth of mutual security as keenly as they share the warmth bestowed by blazing oak as it so brightly dispels the approaching cold.

There are voyages on my mind because there are those years locked there: years when I was working on the water. In those days, mid-October along this northeastern Atlantic was a time for taking small boats from their summer stations and moving them to the safer harbors of their winter work. Delays could be costly. Wait too long, temporize too much, procrastinate too energetically and November would turn the corner, coming at you with the merciless cold and sudden snowstorms of its grim, grey presence.

No, it had to be October if your boat was less than thirty feet and not designed or built to absorb the shock of heavy, winter seas. I would pick the day, watching the weather, waiting for a stable time. In this corner of the nation, October offers delightful stretches of crystal sky and brilliant sun. The spells move in with ridges of high barometric pressure—the prevailing systems of the season, gathering sinew for their winter work. You know the days. They are, in many ways, the essence of New England—electric in their clarity, charged with excess energy. These are the days that can move even the laziest of souls toward a pile of logs that must be split or a bushel of apples that must be pressed.

For such earth-bound duties, the northwest wind that rides with the barometric highs as inevitably as day follows dawn is no problem. Instead, it is part of the blessing. In its fresh and vigorous breezes is part of the excitement of the season; the nor'westers keep the bugs away, fill the house with fresh fragrances, and cool the log-splitter's brow even as he works.

For autumn voyagers, the winds are a different sort of presence; there are two sides to brisk winds of October's finest days, and to see the other, you must be voyaging on a small boat in the open sea. A sailor who chooses these times knows there need be no fear of fog; the visibility on such days is spectacular. Nor will there be troubles with rain, unexpected wind shifts, squalls nor any of the other generally dismal events that so often dog so many mariners.

The October highs are a fair skies guarantee; they also promise wind. I have no boats to move across the Sound, nor any to bring back from the islands, or sail from Point Jude to Montauk, but whenever I wake on one of these crystal mornings I find myself thinking that if I did, today would be the day. Then, while most of the rest of you are helping children off to school or planning a pumpkin pie, I am voyaging.

Fine poetry and wondrous prose are filled with tales of sailors alone at sea, but there was no amount of reading that could have prepared me for my October journeys on the northwest wind. The sea is always a lonely place, but the mid-autumn waters of the north Atlantic are more lonely than most. I can still feel the shiver that came over me when I looked around—for miles in that spectacular clarity—and could see nothing but whitecaps spinning of the tops of emerald waves. With some of winter's weight already gathered in the cooling sea, those same waves kept the boat rising, falling, sliding and sometimes pounding while I hung there on the tiller, watching for the harbor markers and hoping that the boat stayed shipshape until then.

On such voyages, it is yourself you discover. You find your fears, your frailties, your hopes, and the stubborness of your will. You can also revel in the sense of accomplishment that is there to be enjoyed when the winter harbor is reached and the boat is out of harm's way for yet another season.

183

That's what I remember these October mornings when I look out at the whitecaps on the green sea. I look out and wonder if I could still make those voyages.

A Foot on the Gas vs. Two on the Street

AS ANY tourist soon discovers upon entering Boston, a state of war exists between the city's pedestrians and the drivers (sic) of its automobiles. What the visitor does not know—and what every local schoolboy learns if he learns anything at all—is that the history of this particular battle is as precise and revered as is, say, the one that took place at Bunker Hill.

It began, as those who chronicle the past are fond of saying, on a day like any other day. The date was July 7, 1914. The weather was hot and humid. Rock Rolling, a burly tradesman, was negotiating a major thoroughfare in his Ford Model T van when he of course increased his speed upon approaching a yellow traffic light. At that precise moment, a striking patron of the arts known as Crystal Waterford was naturally enough stepping from the curb upon noting the "Don't Walk" sign. The resultant collision was heard 'round the world. (Again we speak as would historians.)

Ms. Waterford, being a woman of sturdy build, recovered. So did Mr. Rolling's van, though less rapidly. Nevertheless, the chance meeting of the two forces led to the forming of a pair of groups with totally opposite points of view. Ms. Waterford, a conservative, became the leader of the Society To Organize Pedestrians (STOP). Its purpose, in a nutshell, was to chase the new-fangled horseless carriage out of town for once and for all. But

Mr. Rolling, a progressive, quickly formed the Gasoline Offensive (GO). Its intent, in short, was to literally drive the old-fashioned walker from the scene forever.

"If God had intended Boston to have automobiles," Ms. Waterford once told a cheering throng of followers during a torchlight rally at newly-constructed Fenway Park, "He would have given us radial feet." Mr. Rolling countered during a march on City Hall a few days later. "You can't stop progress," he told his shouting supporters. "Let 'em eat octane."

Today, descendants of the first members of STOP and GO still carry the fight to each other. Skirmishes are fought daily, with the bloodiest confrontations taking place at the point where Washington street meets Summer and Winter streets. But there are other famous battlefields, monuments that are no less noteworthy than are Gettysburg and Appomattox: Park and Tremont, Boylston and Arlington, Commonwealth and Beacon. All are tributes to a proud city.

At STOP's headquarters, located at the precise midpoint of the Freedom Trail, busy volunteers are only too happy to bring you the word with all the zeal of Crystal Waterford herself. "Check both ways before crossing on a green light," is the group's motto. Members are encouraged to avoid crosswalks at all times and are told not to walk on the sidewalk if they can possibly walk in the street.

The office of GO is located in the basement of the Registry of Motor Vehicles building. Dedicated staffers carry on in the spirit of Rock Rolling, and the room is plastered with bumper stickers which proclaim "Honk Now, Brake Later." Visitors are warned that stopping at red lights causes rearend collisions, while new members are required to sign a statement pledging to always turn left from the right lane and vice versa.

To be sure, a misguided peace movement occasionally springs up in the city. So-called "crackdowns" are announced, but to no avail. And whenever the pendulum swings in one direction (i.e., when some deskbound bureaucrat proposes a pedestrian mall), it always swings back the other way (when a know-nothing official suggests a new highway).

In short, there is no end to Boston's war in the streets. As the recorders of the past like to put it, we must continue to learn the lessons of history.

Departures

IT IS November's departures that hurt most—so many departures, so few arrivals. At the end of this month in Maine, I am bereft; the leavings are monumental and complete. Alone, I turn with the stubborn and loyal family that's left to face winter—a presence that will no longer be denied.

The departures have been underway since September. They were scarcely noted in the harvest's profusion. But I watched; I watch more intently as the years turn and departures become a metaphor for the passage of my own time.

In late September the menhaden departed Middle Bay. I can still feel the dash of the cold wind as Sam and I took our small boat off on a voyage across the harbor to inspect the giant arrival of a huge "pogie boat" that had steamed up the channel and set its sweeping nets on one of the last of the menhaden schools. A curt nor'west breeze capped the choppy seas; we could feel the frost in it. The seiner's crew hauled back a stack of empty twine; the whistle on the huge boat blew and out the channel she steamed, headed south where the menhaden had also gone. Sam and I hung on as our skiff rolled in the wake, then we were alone on the bay, anxious to get home and out of the chop.

Bluefish followed the menhaden; in a week or so more, the striped bass had gone. As October shone, the plover gathered; their vast flocks turned in rehearsal maneuvers day after day until one of the circles stretched too far and the birds never returned to the ledge where they had gathered like fall flowers in the sun. The rock was stripped of its winged gentleness and became a dark finger pointing toward the horizon where the birds had gone.

After the plover came the wild ducks, their departure drummed by hunter's guns. All through October on still nights I could hear the ducks talking in the marsh. I think they like to gossip more than sleep and I wondered on my awakenings at the stamina of the hens and drakes who could chatter and gabble into the three o'clock heart of darkness and still be ready to take wing at dawn.

November stilled the chatter. The rime ice that slides across the cove on the first winter night cuts off the migrants' conversation and reminds them that their true business is travel, away from this congealing cove and off to waters where warmth is more reliable. Now, my awakenings are darker and quite silent. I can hear only my own breathing and the crack of the frost that comes after midnight.

As cranky, stubborn and as desperate as I, several knobby blue herons turned to face November. Like old men, they pushed back at pushy time; they behaved as if the ice had not arrived; they waited at the water's turbulent tidal edge where the ice could get no grip and kept their belligerent heads cocked, ready to stab whatever wayward minnow sought the sun in these shallows. But stubborness was not enough. In the end, the gaunt and ghostly birds surrendered their proprietary pride and flew off to become members of the collective heron flocks that gather to the south.

How I love those stubborn herons; how hard it is to see them go. I know they are the last. Before them the ospreys, hawks, warblers, redwings, terns and kingfishers have departed. The garden has been stripped, the leaves have left the trees, the acorns have fallen, the squirrels have nested, the flowers have been pinched by frost, the deer are gone to the deep woods and even the streets of the town are scoured by the cold wind, sleet and the promise of snow.

We are left here in this land, alone. Even the sun diminishes; only the night and ice arrive . . . so many departures, such bitter arrivals. It is at this ending of November and December's first days that the departures hurt the most. There is not winter enough to make spring real, nor autumn enough to sustain.

The sons and daughters are also gone; theirs are the departures most difficult. Not for them, for me. For them, like the circling plover winging past the horizon, there is freedom over the ocean's rim. They could no more stay gathered at this point of land than the plover can spurn the migratory surgings of a skein of centuries.

Since September, I have said goodbyes. Now that November is here, there is no more to be said. The season's departures have each been taken. One by one the pinions have pushed against the Maine winds and our plover have flown. I stand here gray and long legged like the heron, defiant in my solitude, damned if I will let the ice and the departures get me down.

And stubborn I will stay until March when those great gaunt birds return and begin the season of arrivals—a time of return for sons and daughters and ospreys and terns.

Us vs. Them

COUNTRYSIDE / US VS. THEM

All Year 'Round

Do you live here all year round?" asked a visitor to our home on a fine, sunny, summer day. I think the question came because the visitor could not conceive of a place that could enjoy such particular benefits during one season of the year without exacting extreme penalties in winter—too extreme to be endured by any sane family.

We do live where we live the year through. It is the only place we have; it is also the only place we want to be. Winters are not extreme; they are winters, and, like everyone in New England, we cope. Our proximity to the water is no penalty. The same sweeping view that so captivates summer visitors is with us through the year. In the winter, the bay often freezes, presenting a vastly different panorama, but a sweeping one, nonetheless.

The open ocean, on the other hand, does not freeze. From one window in the loft, if I stand in the proper place, I can see the Atlantic, out there about five miles down the bay from our place.

191

Its mighty presence moderates winter's extremes; ten miles inland in January, it can be ten degrees colder than where we are. In the fall, our garden is the last in town to be hurt by the frost.

That's because the ocean holds the heat of summer, gives it up grudgingly over the chilly days of autumn, and blesses us with a balmy reservoir of warmer air that lasts well into February.

It is now that April is here that we must see that debt repaid. With the sun assured of more than twelve hours in the heavens, this Yankee latitude is assured of some April days of honest warmth. Those are the days when gardening plans dominate every thought, the times when canvas covers are peeled from boats, sandpaper is acquired along with the sudden realization that there is a host of spring chores to be completed before the joys of summer can be harvested.

New Englanders know these April mornings. As soon as the sun rises, it brings the softness of spring. As soon as you step out the door, you are overwhelmed with the evidence of gentler days. Whenever I find the most tenuous April evidence, I go bouncing around the soggy lawn, bring down a pair of oars from the barn rafters, stop at the hardware store for more marine paint (forgetting in my euphoria that there are two half-cans left from last April) and spend most of my time at the office thinking about being at home.

But when I do get there, having left "work" an hour or so early to enjoy the late afternoon sun, I am often disappointed. While there was stillness and warmth in the town eight miles from the water where my "work" is, there is a stiff, chill breeze blowing when I reach our point. If I can dress warmly enough to live with the damp rawness of the wind, then I must put up with its continued presence during any outdoor chore. On one such afternoon, this April phenomenon blew enough grit onto the side of my freshly painted dory to ruin the entire job.

I let years go by without understanding the reason for this bane of my Aprils. Spring after spring after spring I would drive home anticipating the blessings of basking only to have my hopes blown away by the wind. At one point I began to imagine myself cursed by some sea witch who set the wind to roaring every time I left the office early.

But, just as there almost always are with natural events of any regularity, there are less mysterious reasons for the April bane. What happens is that the stronger sun, shining on the now snow-less ground of many inland places, heats that ground through morning and early afternoon. By mid-afternoon, the earth itself has absorbed enough warmth to begin heating the air above it. As we learned in Science I, hot air rises.

And that is where my problems begin. The air that rushes in from the water to fill the vacuum left by the rising, inland currents is now colder than other air; it still carries the chill of the sea. The process, as you have certainly deduced by now, takes place most markedly on the days that most move me to plan spring chores—chores, by the way, that no longer get done so early now that I know what brings me spring's cold sou'westers.

Now, when they blow, I cope; and I think of how refreshing the same phenomenon will be in July and August.

CITYSIDE / US VS. THEM

Urbanis Apologensia

THERE IS a conviction abroad in the land which states that if you live in a city you are either 1) black, 2) poor, and/or 3) crazy. It is a concept perpetuated by people whose idea of a city is that it should be open only from 9 A.M. to 5 P.M., and until 8:30 on Monday and Wednesday nights. Since I was not born number 1 above, nor have I yet achieved number 2, my residency in Boston thereby qualifies me for number 3. Or so I'm told.

Well, not really *told*. Suburbanites and ruralites tend not to come right out and imply mental disorder when you inform them you are afflicted with acute urbanism. Instead, a certain knowing frown crosses their faces, while a measured "cluck" makes its way from the front of their concerned mouths. It's a bit like telling people you recently quit your job, more recently got a divorce, or most recently announced your homosexuality. No doubt about it: if you decide to go live in the city, you should expect to be looked upon as pretty much the equivalent of a lazy, wife-baiting fag.

Then, of course, they want to know why. "Wasn't work satisfying?" becomes "Aren't you afraid of crime?" "Wasn't marriage satisfying?" turns into "What about the schools?" "Wasn't the opposite sex satisfying?" comes out "Where on earth do you park?" The conversation usually ends with them saying they'd just love to live in the city, *but*. Liars. What they really mean is they hope you grow out of it.

None of which, you keep telling yourself, should really bother you. Certainly it is not worth pointing out to these meddlesome souls that while allegedly being "raised" in the suburbs you found life there about as fascinating as a bowl of okra. Or that you believe the "back-to-the-country movement" holds equal legitimacy with a peasant dress purchased at Saks. No need to get nasty. Live and let live.

On the other hand, such incessant queries can eventually create a strange and mysterious condition. Knowing they are coming, the city dweller begins to answer annoying questions before they are asked. He or she slips slowly at first, then starts to take out membership in a collection of paranoiac human beings which is increasing in great number across the American landscape.

I am speaking of the *Urbanis apologensia*.

You have no doubt met us raving apologensia. We are often invited to cocktail parties beyond the city limits, but instead of arriving in Ford station wagons fresh from two-car garages, we turn up in Datsuns battered by nights of inclement weather. We are not set off so much by our appearance, however, as by our hopeless and admittedly unwarranted inclination to defend the fact that we live in the city. We do not even give you a chance to slide into your routine before we shuffle into ours.

"Say," someone will open, "I understand you live in Boston, and . . ."

My warning antennae buzz. "Yes," I reply quickly. "Small car. Never been mugged. No kids. Red Sox. Step around the dog mess."

"I beg your pardon?"

"That's right. Drive against the commuter traffic. Ritz bar. *Your* taxes are just as high. Dirty streets in other towns, too. Walking distance. Noise isn't as bad as you think. Good restaurants."

"But . . ."

"No buts. Great museums. The Public Gardens. More drugs in your kid's school than in my whole neighborhood. Esplanade. Problem is Massachusetts drivers, not Boston drivers. It may be screwed up, but it's the oldest subway in America."

"Hey, I'm . . ."

"Give them a quarter, they're harmless. Grocery shopping in the North End. No one forces you to go into a strip joint. You don't think there are hookers in the suburbs? Gas lamps on Beacon Hill. I don't like tall buildings, either."

"Well, sure, but . . ."

In short, pity the poor apologensia. We can go on like that for hours, even to the point of ruining entire evenings for unsuspecting conversationalists of the best intentions. More than part of the problem, of course, is the news media. Lord knows I've been well indoctrinated in the man bites dog theory of reporting events, but I would still like to see this headline someday: "598,892 Bostonians not beaten, robbed."

But no. The city is perceived by non-city folks to be filled with unspeakable horrors, and the apologensia must bear their heavy load. It is so unthinkable that someone would choose to city dwell (blacks, poor people and crazies, remember?), that a whole generation of sputtering neurotics is being created, running around defending their way of life at every turn. Well, listen, if you treat someone like a crazy, don't be surprised if he acts like a crazy. And remember this: Some of my best friends are *Urbanis apologensia.*

195

Bright Hordes

BY THE silent thousands and tens of thousands, the fish are moving now. In one of this region's most massive unseen migrations, the great schools of striped bass, spiny dogfish, blowfish, alewives, shad, sturgeon, herring, menhaden and other finny creatures of the east coast ocean have already begun to make their way from the Chesapeake and the Hudson, along the New Jersey and Long Island beaches, around the point at Montauk, across Block Island Sound to Rhode Island's brief and busy coast and from there to Martha's Vineyard, the Cape, and finally to the Gulf of Maine and as far north as the waters off Nova Scotia.

The bright hordes flow like rivers, curving to follow the lacy patterns of this irregular and varied coast. These armies travel quietly and all but invisibly. Unless you know what to look for—a slick spreading on a wind-ruffled surface, the splash and swirl of feeding bass, a patch of deeper blue just beneath the blue-green sea, or a flock of gulls following the travelers below—then the march of silver millions will pass your doorstep with never a sound and you will be none the wiser.

Unless you are a fisherman. They know, and they are ready, waiting with the impatience that only these long and fishless winters can spawn. By the first of May, the crew I used to fish with had given up every pretense of working at any winter job. It was the end of house painting, the end of carpentering, the end of clamming and boat building. We were back on the beach, in the boats, mending nets, hauling seine, setting gill nets, driving trap stakes, repairing gear and trying to decide if we could get through the coming season with the same leaky waders that had served so marginally the past fall that now seemed such a distant time. How well I remember my joy when I cleaned the last paint brush, knowing that the following dawn I would be breathing salt air instead of turpentine.

196

What a fine release there was in feeling the sea surge under the dory, in knowing that the waters beneath teemed with an incredible dimension of life. Nowhere is there a more dramatic statement of the awesome fecundity of nature as there is at this edge of the North Atlantic—so stunned by winter, and then, suddenly, so cloudy with the spawn of a trillion creatures, so rich with the glisten of a billion silver scales, so abundantly blessed with an explosion of the myriads of tiny organisms that are the start of every food chain. On the water, we could feel the blossoming around us and were always awed by it.

It has been some time since I have been back to those beaches, but my head and heart return at every May's beginnings; the echoes of my past enthusiasms, the memories of the seasonal release can never be forgotten. The May migrations were too exciting then, and the knowledge that they still continue are the seeds of my renewed excitement now.

But this year, for the first time in my considerable span, there is a shadow over my visions, a dark pall that clouds my May anticipations. Not since the beginnings of their fishing nearly three centuries ago have the Hudson River fishermen ever been prevented from harvesting the migratory schools of striped bass that have wintered in the depths of that great river. But this May there can be no bass taken.

Man has poisoned the fish with polychlorinated biphenyls (better known as PCBs) and the state's official agencies have declared consumption of the Hudson River stiper too great a risk to be allowed. In a declaration reminiscent of the Greek tragedies, the riverside industries which cast the PCBs upon the waters have said they can see no way they can stop without closing plants and erasing jobs. It would appear, then, that the fate of the bass has been decided by whatever irrevocable fates move us to such excesses.

How strange it is that we fail to see that Man's fate is also inextricably at stake. The deed cuts much deeper than it might appear. Beyond the troubled New England fishermen who wait for a faltering and doubtful migration in this bright and warming May, and beyond the hair-splitting debates over how parts per PCB millions it takes to poison a child, and beyond the false anxieties over what is and is not economic, beyond all these and all the other endless bickerings, there is the elemental fact that Man in his ignorant arrogance has tainted the wild and wonderful purity of a May migration that has been occurring since this planet and its oceans were born.

How can any of us be aware of the miracle of this migration and not also know that any tainting of it is a sin against humankind and a mortal wounding of the planet. It must not be allowed, no matter what.

CITYSIDE / US VS. THEM

Why Can't I Get Mugged?

SOMETHING IS terribly wrong.

I can't get mugged.

After living in Boston for more than a decade, after ten years of walking the streets of a city wherein we are repeatedly informed that the crime rate is going up and up and up, I remain unrobbed, unknocked to the ground and even unpickpocketed. Listen, I can't even get *burgled*. (I did have a car stolen off the streets of Boston once, but I'm not sure exactly how. It hadn't been operable for three days.)

Statistically, this is impossible. All you have to do is read your morning newspaper to know that people who live in Boston get mugged at least once a week. Suburbanites just know it happens to city folks as frequently as going out for groceries. Why, some urbanites get mugged so often they become mug-drunk and have to be sent away to the country, where crime doesn't exist. If you don't believe it, just read the papers.

For a while I thought my problem was that I was being mistaken for a mugger by other muggees. As everyone realizes muggers have telltale characteristics that distinguish them from muggees—scars, leather jackets, funny accents and the like. This is particularly important in areas where the mugger population is out of control to the point where muggers are a threat to each other because they so outnumber the muggees. In some cities, it has been revealed by the television networks, there are mugger ghettos.

Which indicates the desperation of my plight. There is nothing quite like going to a party outside the city and not being able to produce a first-hand mugging account. Recent muggees tend to behave a lot like recent hospital cases, always comparing notes as if they were talking about open heart surgery. ("My mugger used the buddy-can-you-spare-a-dime approach and followed it up with a double hammerlock." "Well, *my* mugger didn't believe in that method.") So people are always shocked when I turn up at non-urban social gatherings without my head wrapped in blood-stained bandages. Many have been the disappointed hosts or hostesses who had requested my presence as a token muggee, only to see me arrive without the aid of crutches.

I'm obviously going to have to do something to get myself mugged, and fast. If I'm touching the pulse of the people properly, no one believes you when you say you live in Boston and have never been mugged. "G'wan," they say, "we see it all on TV. You must live in Topsfield or something." It's getting to the point where I'm afraid to stay in at night. What's this country coming to when a man and his family can't live in danger?

Should I try walking very slowly across Boston Common at three o'clock in the morning? It has, after all, been reliably confirmed by the news media that there has not been anyone other than a mugger on the Common at such an hour since April 23, 1953. Perhaps I should attend a rock concert at Boston Garden while wearing my wallet on a chain around my neck. This would save the teenage gang, which according to news reports would attack me on sight, the inconvenience of having to deftly slice my pocket with a knife. I must remember to wear a tear-away clasp to minimize problems.

Or how about walking into a bar in the Combat Zone and paying for a drink with a $100 bill? Naturally I would have to be sure not to put away the change (assuming there was any) too quickly. I could rustle it around a bit, and make sure lots of people see me leave. I mean, why else do they call it the "Combat Zone"?

And although I manage to survive a dozen or so rides on the MBTA each week, I've obviously got to begin carrying a purse. Men's liberation has put this ploy within reach of all of us, thereby putting more attractions within reach of fervent hands. This is another job for the tear-away strap, while reading a book and looking positively distracted are also suggested. It goes without saying that standing near the door is a must.

In any case, waiting for them to come to me simply isn't working. I don't know what I'm doing wrong, but I do know the next time you get mugged in Boston you would be doing me a favor by telling your assailant to look me up. After all, America's cities have a reputation to live up to. It also occurs to me that one thing that might help is spending more time actually worrying about getting mugged. For example, I know an elderly gentleman who used to regularly cut the "police blotter" section out of his newspaper in order to better remind him what evils lurk in the city. He repeatedly recited its litany of crime as proof positive that urban living was folly. He did this right up until the day he was mugged. Which, incidentally, wasn't too long after he started clipping the paper.

High Tiders and Low Tiders

THE TIDES surge in relative solitude through the fall, winter and spring—seasons when all but the hardiest of us leave the sea, the bays and the beaches for the fireside and other warm shelters less exposed to the wind, rain and snow. Only the fishermen—clammers, wormers, lobstermen, trawlers and long-liners—plus a handful of zealots who surf through January in wet suits, are likely to be found close enough to the open water to be chilled by salt spray. But, now that June is here, the reaches of open sand that run from Cape Cod to Roque Island way down east become crowded places, packed with urban and suburban escapees who find one of their most satisfying summer experiences on a few square feet of beach.

Most beach-goers watch the tide tables, listen to the tidal advice of radio and television weathermen, or, at the least, ask around about the time of the tides. Their purpose is to allow their beach time to coincide with high tide, especially here in Maine where an average of nearly ten feet of swimming depth can be gained or lost as the moon tugs at the earth's oceans. There are too many jokes about the first-time Maine visitors who come to the beach one weekend, return a week later at the same time, and wonder where all the water has gone. I won't repeat any of them, but I cite their awesome popularity to underscore the effect a ten-foot tide can have on a gently sloping beach: it can, indeed, change its entire character—at low tide, a seascape becomes a landscape.

This is the condition the tide checkers try most often to avoid. If they all had their choice, they would elect to be at the beach near the top of the flood tide, when the water is best for swimming and bathers don't have to slap-slap their bare feet across a hundred yards of mud or sand flat before they can wet their ankles.

Which is alright with me; it means fewer visitors will be on the beaches at low tide—a time that I find infinitely more varied and fascinating than the flood. I would rather walk the long, sea-swept stretches of open sand than dunk myself in the ten feet of water that covered them six hours before. I find a continual source of enchantment and wonder in the patterns the tide has cut in the flats, and I ponder often on whether the folks who visit beaches only at the top of the tide ever realize what they are missing.

Just the simple miracle of the curves, whorls, arches and waves that the tide has left is enough to keep me delighted for hours. There is a monumental symmetry to the designs tidal currents leave behind, yet no two are ever quite the same, even if the tides that have done the sculpting are a mere twelve hours apart.

Sometimes, most often on inclined beaches on the open sea, the clean, wet sand is etched with a diamond design as precise as any that could be found on a draftsman's board. Each diamond is equal to the next, each line is cut flawlessly into the sand, and the diagonals run the width of the entire bank in a kind of natural artistry that no human could emulate on such a scale. Other times, along the bottom of tidal channels, what had been soft, almost liquid sand, becomes so hard it jars running feet, and so convoluted with the rolling humps of its curving design that it is all but impossible to tread on it comfortably.

If a shell, or a strand of feathery seaweed, has been trapped in the convection of the curves, the object, however fragile, is given a larger signature by the tidal currents. What might be a relatively nondescript fragment of a clam shell—broken long ago when the clam was dropped by a hungry gull—becomes a kind of flowing flower, blooming in the sandy garden. As the water moved over the shell's irregularities, it was diverted in exotic ways that left their imprint in the beach as delicately as a drawing in stone on the side of an Indian temple.

I have seen the clouds of a mackerel sky echoed in sand prints left by the tide, and even the winged flight of the terns is occasionally mirrored in the sweeping arcs an ebbing bay has carved in the bars and flats. Every time I share such spectacles, I wonder how beachgoers can wait through a fall, winter and spring, and then miss the beach at low water.

You Take Grass, I'll Take Asphalt

WHEN YOU come right down to it, I think the real reason I live in the city lies in the fact that bricks don't have to be mowed and asphalt doesn't have to be raked. At this very moment, out across the non-urban landscape, dozens of "garden centers" are gleefully anticipating an onslaught of masochists in hot pursuit of hedge clippers and fertilizer. Somewhere along the line the American dream has come to be represented by nothing more than green-on-green turf. You gotta have *a yard*. Which has always bewildered those of us who consider yard work to be the biggest waste of man's time since the invention of golf.

During my own suburban upbringing I came to dread April even more than the opening of school in September. Actually, I was fortunate. Until I reached my teens we rented part of a three-family house, the yard of which was tended by a man known only as Riley. Every week or so, Riley and his helpers would descend from a faded red pickup truck and more or less vacuum the place. Sometimes I would fetch bottles of water for them, and as they drank it in huge gulps I would notice that their work did not seem to give them much pleasure.

At the age of fourteen or fifteen, I learned why. We moved into our own house and, dammit, that meant our own yard. The place was a jungle, a veritable rain forest. It would not have surprised me to have walked out the back door and met a Bengal tiger. I swear you could actually get down on your hands and knees and watch the grass grow. For my parents, of course, the yard represented upward mobility. But what did I know of sociology? For me the endless greenery meant only the demise of something I had come to know and love: the weekend.

We could never catch up. In November we were still running around attempting to keep the grass trimmed. In January we

203

were frantically trying to bag the last of the leaves. It was like fighting a monster that grows two arms for every one you cut off. What made it worse was the fact that we had somehow moved into a neighborhood where everyone else seemed to have a truckful of Rileys to do their cutting and bagging for them. I enviously watched these platoons sweep through the yards around us, and it wasn't long before I swore that I would some day be wealthy enough to employ such saviors or smart enough not to have a single blade of grass within fifty feet of my home. That day has come, and I am not wealthy. But I am very smart.

For all I know, lawn mowers now have jet engines. I haven't gone near one in years. My weekends from April until November are not spent acquiring calluses which heal just in time for the following April. There are public parks and flower beds in my neighborhood, should I get the sudden urge to be surrounded by outdoor horticulture. Which happens quite frequently, since I remain an admirer of most things green. It's just that I couldn't bring myself to rake a leaf even if I was told it was the last, pitiful one to fall to earth. Why not just leave it there?

Certain people derive great pleasure from mowing and raking, I know. But certain people also derive great pleasure from shoplifting, which doesn't make it an admirable undertaking. No, give me the bricks and mortar of the city. Listen, give me the woods if you insist. Or even a vegetable garden. Just don't put me in the same backyard with bluegrass, forsythia, or maple leaves. At least not if you expect me to do anything about them. Call Riley instead.

Night Sounds

"WHITE SOUND" is the latest accoutrement for the hotel or office building that has everything. As I understand this latest technological blessing, it is a sort of quiet noise—a steady hum at an acceptable frequency which overrides random noise. The theory is understandable: faced with the choice of working and/or resting in an interior space disturbed by the occasional drop of a coffee cup, the vigor of a curse, the bleat of an auto horn, or the off-tune secretarial humming of "Smoke Gets In Your Eyes," efficiency experts have determined that a sound which steadily obliterates all of these (and more) is preferable. Indeed, such a "white sound" can help with concentration, or lull an insomniac to sleep.

I'm not certain, however, that it would work for me. I find myself sitting upright in bed whenever television programming ends for the day, the "Star Spangled Banner" has been played, and the set begins to emit that wavering hum of TV oblivion. It is "Kojak" and Carson that send me off to sleep as quickly as if I overdosed on nembutal; it is the white sound of the hum that wakes me.

Besides, I like the noises I hear at night and the sounds that penetrate my office window. Contrary to the general impressions of most folks in the city, the countryside is never still; it's a different set of sounds, that is certain, but, like the city, rural days and nights are set to background sounds as varied as the seasons and as rich as any 42nd Street symphony.

These mid-November nights—which most folk would imagine to be as still as a cave on the moon—are often so noisy that I cannot get back to sleep, even after the "hum" has been silenced. It is the talking of the ducks that wakes me. They gather by the thousands in the cove close to our home. The underwater real estate must be rich in whatever it is wildfowl like to eat best at this time of the year. The cove is just to the west of our bedroom window; if there is a westerly breeze to carry the gabbling, our chamber resounds with the conversation of scores of black duck hens, the sibilant whistle of goldeneye wings and, every now and then, the calling of geese as they fly by moonlight.

I'm certain there are doubters among you. The notion that a family could sleep so close to a place wild enough to attract such normally elusive birds is a notion that strains credibility. But, believe me, it is true. And when I wake to hear that raucous "Quack, Quack, Quack," of the black duck, I lie there and smile—a reaction I never experienced when the noise that aroused me was the clang of a dropped garbage can or the unholy rasp of a truck shifting through its gears.

If I were a prisoner in our home (which wouldn't be such a dire fate at that) I could keep track of the seasons' turnings by listening carefully to the night sounds. I could, and have, hear proof of the imminent spring whenever the foxes call. Have you ever heard the courting call of a red fox? Once you have, you'll never forget it. The sound is as far from a croon as a sound can get. It is a cry from the depths of the damned, a shriek that sets children's hearts thumping and strums the threads of terror still woven in the human soul. It is wild enough, weird enough to send a city person scurrying for the safety of the subway. For me, it means that even though the ground is still frozen, spring is sure to come.

And when it does, there is the squawk of the great blue heron to herald it. I have yet to comprehend how the great blue fishes at night; I think the birds must find their prey in the natural phosphorescence a moving fish can make. But I do know the birds guard their fishing territories from dusk till dawn, and the hoarse cry of warning the bird gives to intruders is loud enough to waken the deepest sleeper. I am always pleased when I hear it for the first time because I know the bay is once again fertile with the fish of summer.

Even in the depths of winter, there is no surcease from country sounds. As December waxes and January waits, the bay's icy shield is held against the cold. When the tides race beneath it, the vast slabs move, groan, thunder and crack. It is a sound of such massive and elemental proportions that all humans who hear it comprehend their place within the natural plan.

That is the countryside's white sound, and it is more favored here than any white sound technology has spawned.

Facing the Up-Country Media Blitz

MY FRIEND Sam is at it again, and this year we just might lose him for good because of it. This is an annual event, this near brainwashing of Sam. I know it has arrived when he sits on the living room floor of his fourth floor walk-up, surrounded by magazines and prattling on about such things as "energy-efficient solar options." This means Sam is once again thinking of moving from the city to the country, even though he half believes he will fall off the edge of the earth if he ventures beyond Watertown.

And who can blame him for his reverie? It takes a stronger man than Sam to resist the seductions of the journalistic sales staff which is employed to peddle the alleged virtues of the hinterlands. Bombarded by flashy magazines protraying country living as a chic combination of pickups and Pendeletons, what city slicker among us is above being tempted to chuck organization in favor of the sweet smell of composting toilets or the untold pleasures of building a rabbit hutch? The city doesn't stand a chance in the face of such a media blitz.

These pro-country periodicals make rural life sound like little more than going to a town meeting every March and filling in the rest of the year by taking occasional spins with the boys in the volunteer fire department.

207

Sam's floor is littered with issues of *Country Gentleman, Country Journal, The Mother Earth News,* and *Yankee.* His second string consists of *Down East, Maine, New Hampshire Profiles,* and *Vermont Life.* He pores over them long into the night these days, occasionally taking a break to leaf through his Brookstone and L. L. Bean catalogues. (Bean recently won a prestigious fashion award, after all, and Sam always likes to be in style.) Titles such as *How to Raise a Pig Without Buying Feed* and *Worm Your Livestock* leave him breathless with anticipation. Visions of products with names like Naturade, Powerhoe, and Weed Eater dance in his head. He looks forward to long hours of garden tilling or showshoeing, days that will end with corn popping atop the wood burning stove in the kitchen of his log house a few moments before the kerosene lamps are snuffed out and the patchwork quilt is pulled over his head.

"How will you make a living?" I ask Sam.

"I think," he replies, "that I shall become a bio-dynamic homesteader."

But of course. Life is just a bunch of ruffled curtains, right? Once you learn *How to Build and Use a Root Cellar* or *How to Buy a Milk Goat,* the rest is easy.

Luckily, Sam has never gotten beyond the reading stage. Not yet anyway. I can't imagine what he would do if confronted by a blizzard on Easter morning or frost on Labor Day. He does not strike me as a man who would enjoy the mud season at all. Nor do I think he would care for a case of cabin fever, not to mention the joys of cutting cordwood or the gentle chirping of snowmobiles. I suspect he might also be put off by having only one movie theater in town, particularly when there was no way to get to it.

If all the Sams who apparently read these selling-of-the-country magazines actually up and *moved* to the country . . . well, the country would soon be the city and vice versa. To prevent such an occurrence, of course, some smart publisher could launch the likes of *City Journal* or *Urban Gentleman.* Just think: stories such as *Recycling Apartments* or *How to Raise Hogs on Your Patio.*

In the meantime, Sam will dream his dreams of pressing apple

cider and preserving wild game, all the while not knowing a
McIntosh from a pheasant. At $56.30 per year for subscriptions,
the cost is less than a half dozen milk goats.

One Who Stayed On

THERE ARE millions in this Vacationland who have cities on
their minds. For them, the summer is winding down. Plans for
school are being made; the inevitable shopping trips must be
scheduled. Within sight on camp and cottage calendars are the
dates when the exodus must begin, the plumber must be called,
the boat hauled out and the last clams dug.

As a city-born and city-bred country dweller, I know the poi-
gnant moments well. There is a yearning that aches when the
finality of a shoreside summer is irrevocably encountered. No
matter how determined the effort to postpone such recognition,
the time comes when the end is inescapable. It may arrive on an
evening when the clarity of autumn steals off the water on a
northwest breeze; or it can come with the chill of a late August
dawn when the fire feels good in the face of an unaccustomed
cold.

I endured too many of those moments. The wrench, at last,
became too painful. I simply never permitted the inevitable end to
arrive, but stayed in the country, by the sea, and let Labor Day
pass, then Thanksgiving, Christmas and on into my first full year
that had no endings in it. Instead, there was the full circle of
country life—365 days of making a living fishing, clamming,
house painting and honest-to-goodness ditch digging.

That was more than thirty years ago; I am here still. Yet I have
never forgotten the farewells I had to make—goodbyes to the
bay's flashing whitecaps, to the vital fish that filled my summer

209

days, to the wondrously expansive beaches that seemed to stretch from one end of my summer world to the other, and to an inner realization that I had never found the fulfillment anywhere that I had found at the oars of a dory or on the deck of a catboat tacking in a southwest chop.

So, in effect, I finally indulged my yearnings, avoided those goodbyes and never left the sight of the whitecaps or my nearness to the beach. In my view (and it would be well nigh impossible for me to admit I had made a mistake in this fundamental decision) I also found the fulfillments that had been presaged on those summer holidays. Whatever is the sense of my identity it has been built in the country, evolved from natural realities and became established within the rhythms of the seasons. I have emerged from those thirty-plus years with a fundamental belief in the need to recognize natural truths and to attempt to learn some harmony with them.

And, having been so blessed, I have also come to share even more the August sadness of those millions of urban and suburban dwellers who, even now, are making the same goodbyes I made more than three decades ago. Perhaps to ease my guilt (if that, indeed, is what it is) at having pulled up my urban roots and abandoned my birthplace, perhaps because I am convinced a sense of natural order is so crucial to fulfillment, I want those millions helped somehow to make their goodbyes less final, to somehow be able to extend the natural graces of a country summer through each of the other three urban seasons.

With something like 90 percent of the nation's citizens living in the urbs and suburbs, a total transfer to the country would be impossible. The beaches would have to be paved, the dunes bulldozed for roads. Moving millions would merely make cities of the places where now there are none.

However, the reverse is surely possible. More of the country can surely be restored to the cities, and (in my view) the cities would surely benefit from the transfer. As I see it, it was the obliteration of nature by urban designers (who operated with a faith in man-made technology rather than acknowledging the inevitability of natural laws) which helped bring our U.S. cities to their present state of near crisis. We have the newest cities in the world; they were planned and built at the height of the industrial age. They are monuments to an era when Man allowed himself the hubris of believing he ruled supreme.

It has become obvious that nature is, at least, an equal partner. Yet nature is scarcely on any city payroll. Parks are seen as a luxury, allowed to slide first whenever budgets threaten. Trees, plants, the wind, the rain, the snow are always intruders, never welcome guests. Which is why so many millions yearn so in August. They know they must leave a world where nature is everywhere and return to places where it can seldom be found.

It is that crushing reality which cities must change if they are to regain their vitality. So don't say goodbye to your country; start working to take some of it back with you, and count on me to help.

CITYSIDE / US VS. THEM

Craig and Carolyn and Beacon Hill and Vermont

CRAIG HAD lived in the city—gosh, how long was it?—nine years? Nine years since college, and he had moved east in a predictable manner: the studio apartment in Brighton had become a one-bedroom apartment in Back Bay, which had become a two-bedroom condominium on Beacon Hill. Somewhere along the way (in Back Bay, to be precise), Carolyn had appeared and they had married. They met at a stocks and bonds seminar and had dinner at the Parker House. He was in commercial paper, she was in real estate. A spectacular honeymoon was planned for Acapulco, but later they remembered only that it rained a lot.

Their condominium was furnished in antiques. There were

211

small dinner parties featuring 1970 Chateau Gloria and Beatles music. During coffee the conversation usually got around to Going Away for the weekend, at which time Craig and Carolyn didn't have much to say. After all, they simply didn't Go Away very much. Craig, in fact, ridiculed the notion. "Why do they Go Away anyway?" he would ask Carolyn after the guests had left. "What do they need that they can't get here in town?"

In time, however, Craig and Carolyn began renting a place on weekends in southern Vermont. It was a friend-of-a-friend type of deal, a renovated farmhouse. The drive was three hours from Boston, but they could arrive on Friday night and be fresh for tennis and bicycling the next morning. Before long, they were spending more weekends in Vermont than in Boston. They frequently invited friends along, friends who didn't Go Away a lot, and everyone marveled at the peace and serenity of the scene. Some of the friends even began scouting the countryside for similar houses. In order to Go Away more often.

During one weekend in Vermont, however, Craig sat down and made a list. It was a compilation of everything he felt he had to accomplish around the condominium when he got back to Boston: stain the roofdeck, replace a lock, call the plumber. And he was falling behind in his errands, too. There never seemed to be any food in the refrigerator during the week and he hadn't been to the dry cleaner in a month. "God," he said to Carolyn as they sat in front of the fire on Saturday night, "maybe we'd better not come up here next weekend. I mean, we've got a million things to do. And don't forget that you were going to wash the car." OK, she answered.

They stayed at home the next weekend and did their chores. But, as Craig was quick to point out, they finished only half of them. Surely they should stay in town the next weekend, too, shouldn't they? OK, Carolyn answered. So they skipped another weekend in Vermont in favor of washing the windows, fixing the stereo turntable and taking the nineteenth-century French clock to a repair shop.

And so it went. They still made the three-hour drive north every once in a while, but not nearly as much. Sometimes only once a month. The landlord watched their infrequent comings and goings from his stone house across the road, and finally decided he'd prefer tenants who would give him a little more regular income. Nothing personal, they should understand. Of course not, they answered. They'd look around for a place with a little more flexibility.

But once they were back in Boston nothing came of it. Oh, they occasionally checked the Sunday newspaper for up-country ads and even made a couple of phone calls. But they promptly forgot about them. There were more dinner parties, more 1970 Chateau Gloria and more Beatles music. Guests still ended the evenings by discussing Going Away and making various plans for trips to the Cape or the Islands. Craig and Carolyn listened impassively, trying to be polite but having nothing to say.

One night after their friends had left, Craig started to laugh. "Will you listen to them?" he said. "How silly can they get? All they think about is Going Away. They spend five days a week talking about the other two days. It's ridiculous." Carolyn nodded in agreement as she dried a Dansk plate. But as she looked around the chic apartment she thought of the small house in Vermont, with its weathered barn and the stream running past the back door. It *was* a nice place, she thought. Of course, it had rained a lot . . .

COUNTRYSIDE / US VS. THEM

Country Giving

MOST THANKSGIVING is pre-Christmas, and pre-Christmas is a time of some strain, to say the least. Oh, I know it's supposed to be easier here in Maine; we don't have to push into crowded urban and suburban department stores to complete an increasingly impossible task: finding the right gift for everyone in the family, not to mention passable gifts for those who aren't. At least city folks like to imagine we don't have to, but, I'm afraid, all too many of us become part of the elbowed throng that presses to consume manufactured merchandise with all the manners of a bunch of sea gulls scrapping over a dead fish on the beach.

I do, and every year I regret it. I wonder why I had not managed to master the wondrous art of giving country gifts. We have, for example, a friend who (with his considerable family pressed into service) taps sugar maples every March. From the buckets of sweet sap, he distills a delicate, Maine, maple syrup which he then distributes in colorful pint jugs the following Christmas. Syrup being what it is (and as costly as it currently is) the gift is a splendid one: authentic, personal, and most enjoyable. There is just one problem—every time I find that jug of syrup under the tree, I wonder why I couldn't have been half as clever about solving this annual problem.

Just imagine, if you will, the luxury of knowing in March that you had completed your holiday chores for the following December—and without charge cards. It is a mind-boggling fantasy, one which I tell myself I will realize next year. But here is next year, upon us, and I am in the precise position I find myself every post-Thanksgiving—with a long list and a short budget.

I have thought, in such dire times, of a kind of mild subterfuge. We have another acquaintance (indeed, a host of them) who is the equal of the syruper; she brings 'round a gaily decorated jar of homemade preserves each December 24, and she has been doing it for more than a decade. This regularity is part of the country Christmas secret. If you know, for example, that your neighbors are going to leave two, hand-dipped bayberry candles on your front porch every Christmas Eve, you don't expect more, and you are quite delighted with what you get.

On the other hand, if I give a fellow a necktie one year, I must find something different the next or he is likely to assume I don't care enough to be thoughtful. What I am considering is one massive buy of an acceptable blueberry jelly—about three gallons would be right, from Hollis Wyman's blueberry processing plant in Milbridge. Then all I'd have to do would be to scout around for some recycled jelly jars, spoon the Wyman produce into each of them, seal the entire two cases with properly crude paraffin caps, embellish with a holly sprig, and a label that reads "Blueberry Jelly—Merry Christmas From All of Us." In the great tradition of country Christmases, we would never be suspected. On the contrary: every recipient would not only assume we had made the jelly on our own steaming stove, but many of them would be positive we had picked the berries with our own flying fingers.

That's the secret, you see. Because so much loving labor is assumed to be behind every one of these kinds of offerings, the stigma of monetary value is quite forgotten. For the price of one bottle of twelve-year-old scotch (the kind you are likely to give to your employer) you can satisfy the needs of two-dozen employers, and each of them will say, "Isn't it great. He made it himself."

I tried something like that once. Instead of doing my Christmas shopping, I went duck hunting. That was many years ago; I was still a boy, and I gave two of the ducks to my father for his Christmas. Properly impressed, he invited a guest to dine on the rare and wild provender. When the guest arrived, however, he found every window in the house open as my father and mother attempted to dispel the odor of concentrated, old fish that the cooking ducks had released. I had known no better; I had unwittingly given my father two of the rankest birds in creation. He, I'm positive, always assumed I had done the deed on purpose.

Perhaps that's why I'm still unable to abandon department store counters even though I know I could dip candles with the best of my country neighbors.

215

City Slickers Will Do Anything to Be Loved

I DON'T KNOW about you, but my favorite recent news story concerned Jerry and Darlene Jenkins of Burlington, Vt. You remember Jerry and Darlene, whose car was stolen during their honeymoon in New York. The Big Apple, apparently cut to the core by this sad tale, responded by showering the couple with fancy room and expensive board. Ol' Jerry and Darlene were living like pigs in slop—as they say in Burlington and its environs—until it was discovered: a) they weren't married, which is not a crime, and b) Jerry had allegedly cashed $2500 in bad checks, which is.

The moral of the story is not that country slickers are slicker slickers than city slickers. Everyone knows that already. The point here is that you can almost hear the wheels turning up north as word of the Jenkinses' attempted ruse spreads through the snow-drifts. "The trouble with ol' Jerry and Darlene," it is undoubtedly being roundly concluded in the parlors of rural folk, "is that they got caught." And pretty soon, as has been the case with those who try to commandeer airplanes, everyone will be trying to duplicate the caper.

You may expect the first such imitator to turn up in Boston sometime around spring thaw. He'll arrive from someplace in Maine with a name like Moosehead or Knowles Corner, and he'll immediately hold a press conference to announce that he was mugged while hurrying along LaGrange street on the way to visit his sick mother. When this story is relayed to the masses, they will react with the same amount of assumed culpability as did New Yorkers when they learned of the Jenkinses' "plight." Our friend from the north will then spend a comfortable Easter in the Ritz Carlton, courtesy of the citizenry, feeling right at home in the close company of Maine lobster etuve au whisky facon du chef served with rice pilaf and artichoke clamart.

The possibilities are endless. Why, here comes a young woman from Georges Mills, N.H., whose purse was snatched while she was riding the Red Line. Since it contained her life savings of $135 and three Jock Scott salmon flies, with which she was planning to take a Laker flight to London, let's all rally 'round and buy her a first class ticket on the Concorde. Oh, and look over there. An elderly couple from Enosburg Falls, Vt., has just been robbed at gunpoint of a week's worth of rutabaga wine. By God, let's not allow them to settle for anything less than a case of Chateau Latour '61 as a replacement. On us, of course.

Alas, we city dwellers are a hopelessly guilt-ridden lot. We have read and heard so many "Fear Stalks the City" stories that we have come to believe them. As a result, we are ashamed of ourselves. The news media flay us without mercy and we don't even have a typist to answer back. In the meantime, we are convinced there is no such thing as crime in the hamlets of Moosehead, Knowles Corner, Georges Mills or Enosburg Falls.

They get the news up there, too. They read the New York Times and the National Enquirer. They see how we suffer our image. They're no fools, and that's why they're coming: families, couples, old folks, kids and anyone else who can get the car or the truck over to the interstate with enough gas in the tank to get it down to Boston. Jerry and Darlene Jenkins simply proved what their neighbors had suspected all along, namely that those good ol' city slickers will do just about anything to be loved.

In Search of Fellow Man

As the young spring matures, the first travellers begin their journeys. Like the wild ducks and geese that gather in the bay—talking noisily in the excitement of their migration north—urban and suburban explorers of the countryside are making their first tentative trips. I see them on the roads, mostly the young at this uncertain time of the year. They are looking, as travellers always have, for the new, the different, the compelling landscape or seascape they can lock in their memory and take back with them.

After twenty years in Maine, I have learned to get ready for the unexpected when the travel season arrives. We came home one morning from a shopping trip downtown to find two youthful travellers setting up their tent in our meadow. They had started a fire, had rigged up a kind of clothesline, and were busy hacking away at some saplings, too green to burn and certainly too handsome to waste.

After some discussion, which included tips on where to find better firewood with less destruction, we agreed they could stay. They seemed so naive, so alone, so unfamiliar with their surroundings that it seemed better to have them where they could be watched instead of allowing them to wander goodness knows where. We have a reasonably large piece of property, most of it wild, cut over and swampy. It seemed beyond the comprehension of these travellers that such an apparently unused place could be "owned" by anyone. I have learned that such perspectives are shared by a good many city dwellers, for whom ownership implies things—cars, television sets, furniture—rather than portions of the open landscapes they drive by in their search for adventure.

Those young men stayed for nearly two weeks. I never understood how they assembled their wherewithal; they must have had some funds and some food when they arrived. Others like them have come every season since, some without ever being detected until after they left and we found the remains of their campsites deep in the woods.

The decision about allowing such travellers to visit is always a difficult one for me, yet I always end up granting them space. Oh, I make demands and set standards about how lightly and carefully the land should be used, but I just can't bring myself to reject out-of-hand the innocent requests of folks so unfamiliar with the country that they can set up a tent in the middle of a meadow without even wondering whose place they are on.

They seem so alone, these travellers—alone in a strange place. It's that quality of their experience that touches me most. They walk tentatively along the shore; they seem surprised when we greet them. They come piling down the dirt road in their cars, baffled when the road runs out and they find themselves in our front yard. They truly don't know where they are, nor do they know anyone they can ask.

For me, that kind of aloneness is awesome. I can remember its immensities from my city days when, often, the anonymity of urban streets would overwhelm me and I would yearn for company, for a familiar face. I'm told there are those who seek this very anonymous quality that I sometimes ran from. More power to them. I have lived in the same neighborhood for eighteen years now, and I find continual reassurance in being known.

It is a reassurance that continues to be nourished even in rural places where I am a stranger. If you drive the back roads of Maine, through the small hamlets that are far from the travelled highways, nearly every person you pass will give you a wave. You may be a stranger, but your shared humanity is recognized. Somehow, the pressures and tensions of the cities do not permit this recognition. In most cases, people pass people on the street without ever allowing themselves to see each other.

I have a feeling that the travellers to this part of the nation, this open and unpeopled countryside, are looking for more than just a view; they are looking for a recognition of their humanity. That's why, as another travel season begins, I know that I, for one, won't turn many of them down.

Park 'n' Lock

I SHOULD HAVE known I was in for trouble in a place named Littleton. During the ride out Route 2 from Boston, and later when I turned off onto Route 2A, I could sense my paranoia level rising. The same feeling used to creep up on me two winters ago during my hopelessly belated attempt to "get back to the country," having missed the trend when it was in vogue a few years earlier. While spending a few weekends in southern Vermont I discovered I simply couldn't sleep. The silence kept me awake.

Anyway, there I was in Littleton. My friends had woods and a pond in back of their house, and the whole scene looked like the watercolor reproductions featured on the calendar my life insurance agent sends me every December. So naturally when it came time to set off on the obligatory late afternoon slosh through the snow—in order to experience the pleasure of drying out after experiencing the displeasure of getting wet—I paused to lock my car.

That set the locals to giggling and pointing, of course. It always does. Watching someone secure his automobile has always been high entertainment in the hinterlands. It's more fun than watching the creeks rise. "Well, gollee," the natives invariably proclaim upon noting such a phenomenon, "you sure must be city folk." As if the last rural car theft involved a new '32 Lagonda.

And yet they were right, in their own unintentional way. I mean, I actually used to lock my car when I got out to check the air in the tires. This would surprise you even more should you gaze upon the object of such fortification, a vehicle which was recently described by an acquaintance as "half car, half traffic accident."

In any case, this is what I pondered during my post-humiliation return from Littleton. In truth, no one had broken into a car of

220

mine for seven years, or since the day I lost a Volkswagen to a gang of cutthroats who converted it into a dune buggy. So what was I worrying about? And who would bother to steal my current transportation system, given the fact it is beyond redemption even as a method of traversing beaches?

No one, as it turns out. This is the conclusion I have come to after following up the Littleton incident with a scientific thirty-day experiment during which I did not *once* lock my car while it was parked within the city limits of Boston. Every morning I leaped from my bed, threw back the curtains and gazed upon the spot where it had last rested. And every morning it was there, untouched by human hands.

Could this be a trend? How well I remember urban living during the 1960s, when vagrants would enter my unlucky VW at will to make a bed out of the green stamps they found in the glove compartment and then go to sleep on them. Is it possible that recent statistics, which showed a marked decline in auto thefts in Boston, are actually to be believed? I admit a month is not a long time, but I can remember the days when sitting in a car in the Hub was no guarantee that the vehicle would not be stolen from under you.

Naturally enough, I can't wait for my next trip to the boondocks to show off my new bravado. Imagine the thrill of pulling up to the gas pumps in front of the combination beauty parlor/ hardware store and being able to find acceptance as one of the boys. And imagine the expressions on their faces when I reveal to them that, shucks, I'm actually a city slicker who doesn't bother to lock his car. That ought to be more fun than a runaway milking machine.

I Should Know Snow by Now

THIS IS my fifty-third year as a human being and my nineteenth as a Maine resident. As a child of New England and an adult in Maine, you'd think by now I'd be ready for the snow when it comes, just as it has each and every December for as long as I can remember. But I am not ready; I never have been, and I begin to wonder now if I ever shall be.

Is it sheer inability to get myself organized? Is it a kind of unrealistic wishful thinking which tends to have me believe that this winter, at last, will be the one that never comes? Or has procrastination now become so traditional that I absolutely refuse to get out the snow tires and recondition my boots until there are three inches of wet, white stuff on the ground?

Likely, it is a combination of all three, plus more odd rationalizations churning in the murky pit of my psyche. It's the same every year. I awaken on a gray December morning and find the window plastered with wet snow, feel the excitement in the air as the children wait by the radio hoping for a "no-school" announcement, and then make my way to breakfast wondering where I put the snow shovels last March. In the bottom of the closet I find my "snow" shoes—the ankle high, fleece-lined leather ones—exactly as I left them: dirty, needing to be oiled and minus proper laces.

Thank goodness there are others in the house more prudent than I. The supply of mink oil has been replenished; the jar waits in the cabinet for me to grab, open and scoop from. Why didn't I do this last March, I ask myself as I rub the good grease into the bent and petrified leather, hard as a rock after nearly ten months of absolute neglect. Socks and mufflers have also been ordered by other hands, the parka is pulled from the back of the closet and I exit cursing all the way to the barn where I know I'll spend at least a half-hour rummaging among the debris in search of one of the five snow shovels that were on hand last year.

How drab the litany of the disorganized. I cannot find the shovels, I cannot find the snow tires that fit, and, when at last I do, there are lines fifteen cars long at the service station. Tools I worked with a few days ago are covered now, lost until they wreck the mower blade next spring. The dory will have to be turned over and cleansed of its drifts; the pile of kindling has become a burial mound under its white shroud and the supply of seaweed gathered so laboriously must now be dug out so it can, finally, be spread over the plot that will be April's garden.

It is not the snow we curse, I decide, it is our own stupidity that chagrins. Because snow, if you are ready for it, is scarcely an inconvenience. If all the wood is gathered, stacked, covered and dry, if the snow tires are in place, if the tools are stored and the seaweed spread, if the shovels are on the porch, the storm windows in, the leaves raked, boots oiled and the ladder tucked safely in the loft, then, ah then the first snow is a gentle miracle to be tenderly enjoyed. If my boots are supple and warm, I can revel in the new, white silence, take note of the feathered trees, mark the brush of the owl's wing beneath the hawthorne and watch the black ducks pitch into the cove under the lee of the pines and birches.

I am, of course, not ready; nor, I suspect, are a good many other Yankees. Country folk with city occupations, they are caught by December's snows and they grumble at the weather, as if the seasons were somehow at fault. Merchants, wise to the follies of such city mice in country clothing, put out more shovels, sell more snow tires, import carloads of mittens, cold remedies and bags of miracle salt that promise to make the snow vanish in the magic of their sprinklings.

There are some folks who never give a glance to such displays. I can show you their houses if you ride with me on the back roads through the fields and woods. You can see great castles of dry wood stacked on the porches, take note of the wooden snow shovels (used for generations) waiting by the door, find proper

223

boots at the base of the coatrack, and spy the tracks of snow tires in the drive. When it snows first in December, these folk scarcely raise an eye to the gray sky. With hardly a shift in their movements, their life proceeds with its customary and impressive order. These are the Maine men and women for whom snow is never a surprise, who have learned over the centuries to prepare for and to accept the natural presences they know and understand.

Why can't I be more like them? And why does every first snow have to make me realize what a long way I must go before I can?

Help Is on the Way

THE STORY was short, but not to be overlooked. It reported that the voters of Sweden, Maine—a hamlet located forty miles west of Portland, as the moose lumbers—had no one to vote for at the annual town election. Quite simply, no one wanted to run for the Board of Selectmen, which is the only thing one can run for in Sweden, Maine.

In Boston, of course, the idea of an office with no one seeking it is unthinkable. This is a town where the names on the ballot frequently outnumber those not on the ballot. Not only that, but candidates are often distinguishable from each other only by their middle initials. Sometimes the inside of a voting booth looks like page 739 of the Boston White Pages, which begins with Cornelius J. Sullivan and ends with Jerome R. Sullivan.

The Maine story has had its effect in Boston, however. It was seen by a number of concerned citizens who felt that towns such as Sweden would soon be lacking a certain something if no one came to their rescue. These people were worried that, with no politicians around, up-country folks might come to the conclusion that

224

the species is unnecessary. This quickly led to the formation of the Public Officials Lending Service (POLS).

The location of POLS headquarters must naturally remain unpublished, lest Bostonians who are outraged at losing a few city councilors be given the opportunity to storm its barricades. The group's leaders have consistently refused to be interviewed full face. Still, we were able to procure a session with the organization's transportation adviser, who spoke to us between frantic telephone calls to the Trailways Bus System as she tried to coordinate the exodus.

The first thing she wanted to make clear, she stated emphatically, was that the rumor that Boston's vice mayor, Edward Sullivan, was being loaned to Thornton's Ferry, N.H., was totally false. We wondered how she could be so certain. "Because Edward Sullivan does not exist," she replied. We found her argument difficult to rebut.

Still, she was willing to reveal certain facts. A small village in northern Vermont was on the prowl for a tree warden, she pointed out. A prothonotary was needed along the coast of Maine. And out in the Berkshires was a community that would pay almost any price for someone to keep track of dog licenses.

But our source went on to explain that it is not always easy to find positions in other communities which are suitable for local leaders. For example, what to do about Kathleen Sullivan and Joseph Alioto, who will travel only as a pair? And then there is poor Kevin Harrington, the Massachusetts Senate president, whose track record as an accountant leaves him in something less than great demand when it comes to keeping track of money.

On the other hand, there is Louise Day Hicks. Not only has she demonstrated a past willingness to run for anything at any time, but she is out of office these days. There is also Mayor Kevin White, whose penchant for travel outside the city is well documented. His honor, in fact, is being considered by POLS as a potential political bigamist, a man who could hold office in more than one place at one time. "Of course," our source pointed out,

225

"he's a bit reluctant to travel by bus. He keeps insisting on a limousine."

We left the offices of POLS knowing that the good people of Sweden, Maine, have nothing to worry about. If they will simply put in an order, it will be promptly and happily filled. If they are not satisfied with their purchase after thirty days, they should feel free to keep the merchandise regardless.

COUNTRYSIDE / US VS. THEM

The Squire's Stride

THERE ARE woods around our home—woods on the land we own and woods on the land of each of our neighbors. It is a relatively sparsely settled portion of the community that surrounds us; nothing like the true wilderness of northern Maine, but quite large enough to get lost in, even though the center of town is a half-dozen miles up the road. Like many of the community's residents, we walked in the woods before we acquired our homesite, disregarding boundaries and considering—as so many do—the expansive tract of green a sort of common land, available for the recreation of all merely because no homes or other people seemed to lay claim to any of it.

The area has changed a bit over the years. A home here, another there, and the woods are not quite as untrammeled by the notion of meets and bounds as they once were. I, for one, regard our woods differently now. Whenever I have the time, and sometimes even when I don't, I walk in our woods with proprietary instead of exploratory steps. I know the boundaries of our bit of mortgaged real estate, and when I walk within them, my tread is certain, my voice loud, and my eye on a constant sweep for the particulars of the terrain.

Mine might be called the squire's stride, and in keeping with my

226

position as one of the owners of these woods, I have made some effort to research the history of this verdant patch. Recent history has been relatively easy to obtain. Even such a mundane spot as the assessor's office in our town building provided me with aerial photographs of our woods taken about forty years ago. I was surprised, and somehow deflated a bit, to look them over and realize that our woods were not woods at all back in the Thirties. They were, instead, pasture land on what was then a prosperous farm. The farmhouse is quite clearly defined in the photograph, and cows graze in an open field precisely in the same location where I now walk imagining I am about to meet a moose or bear in these, some of the last wild forests of our town.

My squire's stride has all but walked past the truths of recent history. In my romantic urge to escape to honest wilderness, I prevaricate a wildness that history is quick to deny. These are not ancient woods where I walk, but instead pastures so recently overgrown with trees that had I visited this place as a boy, I could have raced through grass and clover, past barns and into the tended yards of the town's leading farmers.

But how quickly the trees have taken over. I find cellar holes now where the farmhouses once stood, and birch, popple, swamp apple, and pasture pine where hayfields used to spread. Instead of cows, there are, in truth, moose and deer, raccoons, grouse, and all manner of small, big-eared creatures who leave lacy tracks as fine as embroidery in the new snow. I can, if I want, forget the farms of the recent past and busy myself with dreams of clearing the land and making it productive. How I am not certain. I have dreamed of cranberries, wild rice, Black Angus beef, Nubian goats, or other exotic livestock which will not only feed us all but bring us a nice dividend at harvest time.

Of course, no such enterprise ever gets beyond my dreams. Our woods are safer now from disturbances of any kind than they have been since the Indians camped here and set forests on fire so room could be made for blueberries. I will not set axe to tree for the sake of a ship's ribs or a barn's ridgepole. I will not pull stumps

227

so heifers can graze. I do not even take the windfalls for firewood, although every year I promise I will and tell myself I must.

All I do is walk in the woods in an aimless sort of proprietary haze, marveling at the clarity of a deer's hoofprint in the mud or the booming of a grouse from the alders. That's all I do except for one day of the year, and that day is drawing close. It is the time when my squire's stride takes me, axe in hand, to cut our Christmas tree. What glorious virtue there is in that mission. I am, at last, harvesting from these woods that require attention, but get none from me and instead merely lie about, prospering and covering my footprints with fallen leaves within days of my departure.

CITYSIDE / US VS. THEM

City Chic

For those of us who are counting, 1977 is precisely four weeks minus one day away. Most of us who are counting live in Boston and don't see how a new year can come too soon. The past 340 days have been nothing but trouble, because 1976 will be remembered in my neighborhood as the year Boston became fashionable again.

That's right: City Chic.

We've always had, of course, our so-called "out-of-town visitors." They come to the theater from Newton on Saturday night, to Anthony's Pier 4 from Braintree on Mother's Day, and to Boston Common from Malden at Christmas time. Them we can deal with. But this was something else, this season of hordes crammed into station wagons and buses, all of them determined to snatch up the last remnants of available parking space.

There are various theories as to why suburban and rural folks rediscovered Boston in 1976 as a nice place to visit even though they still wouldn't want to live here. My friend Rupert, a car

228

polisher by trade, points his gnarled finger at the Bicentennial. "I could tell there'd be problems last May when I met a family from Tyngsboro on the Freedom Trail," Rupert recounts. "I'm something of a historian, and I happen to know that there hasn't been a family from Tyngsboro in Boston since September 17, 1947."

Even calculated hysteria couldn't stem the tide. When the Boston Police Patrolman's Association greeted tourists with its now-famous "Fear City" pamphlets—which promised visitors they'd spend much of their free time in Boston being mugged—the throngs only multiplied. If you can't keep them away with the old chestnut about crime running rampant in the streets, what can you do?

"Nothing worked," laments Maude, an elderly acquaintance who is a retired detective. "And then the city had to go and open the waterfront park. I tried to take a harbor cruise one night, you know. It was booked solid with insurance company employees. These were people who normally worry about being caught dead in Boston after dark—literally."

While we're at it, we can also cast a few aspersions at the Boston Symphony Orchestra, the tall ships, and the Queen of England herself. But there can be little doubt the final blow was Faneuil Hall Marketplace. About 100,000 people turned up when it opened at noon on August 26, and as nearly as I can determine they all return every Sunday to celebrate the occasion over pizza and littlenecks. Walking through the market's central corridor on a weekend is like trying to get off a 9 A.M. trolley on the Green Line. There's about as much elbow room as there was in the bleachers of Fenway Park during the 1975 World Series.

"The key is in the number of leisure suits you see around town," explains my friend Mulligan, who makes his living watching professional football games on television. "Leisure suits mean the middle class, because the lower class can't afford 'em and the upper class wouldn't be seen in 'em. And, as any sociologist or mayor will tell ya, the city has been abandoned by the middle class and left to the rich and the poor. So whadda ya gonna do?"

Pray for a better year the next time around, that's what, Mulligan. Hope that psychiatrists in Lincoln will quit discovering restaurants such as Maison Robert. Wish that a trip to the observatory atop the John Hancock Tower frequently resembles an Atlantic crossing during rough seas. If City Chic doesn't hurry up and go away, we'll all have to move to Tyngsboro.